MINING THE WORLD WIDE WEB
An Information Search Approach

THE KLUWER INTERNATIONAL SERIES ON INFORMATION RETRIEVAL

Series Editor

W. Bruce Croft
University of Massachusetts, Amherst

Also in the Series:

MINING THE WORLD WIDE WEB
An Information Search Approach

by

George Chang
Kean University, Union, NJ

Marcus J. Healey
Mobilocity, New York, NY

James A. M. McHugh
New Jersey Institute of Technology, Newark, NJ

Jason T. L. Wang
New Jersey Institute of Technology, Newark, NJ

KLUWER ACADEMIC PUBLISHERS
Boston / Dordrecht / London

Distributors for North, Central and South America:
Kluwer Academic Publishers
101 Philip Drive
Assinippi Park
Norwell, Massachusetts 02061 USA
Telephone (781) 871-6600
Fax (781) 681-9045
E-Mail <kluwer@wkap.com>

Distributors for all other countries:
Kluwer Academic Publishers Group
Distribution Centre
Post Office Box 322
3300 AH Dordrecht, THE NETHERLANDS
Telephone 31 78 6392 392
Fax 31 78 6392 254
E-Mail <services@wkap.nl>

 Electronic Services <http://www.wkap.nl>

Library of Congress Cataloging-in-Publication Data

Mining the World Wide Web : an information search approach / George Chang ... [et al.].
     p. cm. – (The Kluwer international series on information retrieval ; 10)
  Includes bibliographical references and index.
    ISBN 0-7923-7349-9 (alk. paper)
     1. Data mining. 2. Web databases. 3. World Wide Web. I. Change, George. II. Series.

QA76.9.D343 M56 2001
006.3—dc21   2001020368

Printed on acid-free paper.

Printed in the United States of America

*The Publisher offers discounts on this book for course use and bulk purchases. For
further information, send email to <scott.delman@wkap.com>.*

*This book is dedicated
to our teachers,
especially our parents,
for their
encouragement,
inspiration and love.*

Contents

List of Figures

List of Tables

Preface

The World Wide Web (Web), which emerged in the early 1990s, has made great strides in the late 1990s. Its explosive growth is expected to continue into the next millennium. The contributing factors to this explosive growth include the widespread use of microcomputers, advances in hardware (microprocessors, memory and storage) technologies, increased ease of use in computer software packages, and most importantly – tremendous opportunities the Web offers for all businesses. The consequence of the popularity of the Web as a global information system is that it has flooded us with a large amount of data and information. In this sea of data and information, searching for a piece of information is like finding a needle in a haystack. Finding useful information on the Web is often a tedious and frustrating experience. Therefore, new tools and techniques are needed to assist us in intelligently searching for and discovering useful information on the Web.

This book explores the concepts and techniques of *Web mining*, a promising and rapidly growing field of computer science research with great potential in e-business. Web mining is a multidisciplinary field, drawing on such areas as artificial intelligence, databases, data mining, data warehousing, data visualization, information retrieval, machine learning, markup languages, pattern recognition, statistics, and Web technology. Moreover, depending on the type of data and approach used, techniques from other disciplines may be applicable.

We present the Web mining material in this book from an *information search* perspective. In this sense, we focus on issues relating to the efficiency, feasibility, scalability and usability of searching techniques for Web mining. As a result, this book is not intended as an introduction to databases, data mining or information retrieval, etc. However, we do provide enough background information to facilitate the reader's comprehension in each area related to our book.

The first part of the book focuses on information retrieval (IR) on the Web. IR systems deal with the automated storage, retrieval, organization, and representation of documents. It is widely used in libraries and government agencies where a large amount of document storage and retrieval is necessary. Research on IR includes categorization, classification, filtering, modeling, query language, system architecture, user interface, etc.

IR mainly deals with natural language text that is often either not structured or semistructured in nature. Consequently, the semantics of the text may be ambiguous. In contrast, data retrieval tools in a database management system (DBMS) deal with structured data that is semantically well defined. As long as a record satisfies a user's query defined by a regular expression or relational algebra, it will be retrieved by the DBMS.

Although DBMSs provide a satisfactory solution to data retrieval, they do not provide users with search by topic or by subject. IR systems are an attempt to answer the shortcomings of data retrieval systems. Their main goal is the retrieval of documents relevant to a specific topic or subject according to the user's information need. Thus, the notion of relevance is at the heart of an IR system. Since IR systems must interpret the user's query, retrieving as few irrelevant documents as possible is also their primary goal.

We dedicate the first part of the book to IR techniques because of their importance in Web mining. Searching is fundamental to mining useful information and knowledge in any media type. Having the ability to find relevant documents on the Web is an essential process in Web mining. The cleaner the data set, the better the information and knowledge that can be extracted from it. In this part, keyword-based and multimedia search engines, query-based search systems, and mediators and wrappers are discussed.

The second part of the book reviews data mining (DM) on the Web. DM, which emerged during the late 1980s, has made a great impact in both academia and industry in the 1990s. Commercial products have appeared as a result of many years of research prototype development.

In reality, DM is one of the steps in the evolution of information technology. The main reason that it has gained attention in industry and scientific research is because of the vast amount of raw data that has been accumulated over the past several decades. Putting these huge quantities of data to good use is the objective of data mining.

DM, sometimes called *knowledge discovery in databases* (KDD), refers to the extraction of knowledge from large amounts of data. DM has many stages including data cleaning, data integration, data filtering, data transformation, pattern recognition, pattern analysis, and knowledge presentation. Traditionally, DM techniques have been applied to data warehouses, relational databases, and transactional databases, where data are well structured and semantically well defined. In principle, DM techniques can be applied to any kind of information repository.

The Web is a distributed repository linked by millions of hyperlinks embedded in hypertext documents called HTML. This large repository of information provides many opportunities for DM. Unlike relational databases with structured, well defined semantics, the Web is semistructured in nature. Therefore, in order to apply data mining to the Web, previous relational data mining techniques require modification or new techniques must be invented.

In the second part of this book, basic concepts on data mining are first introduced. Topics on text mining, Web data mining, and Web crawling are then discussed, respectively.

The last part of the book is a case study. The case study focuses on a domain specific search engine prototype called EnviroDaemon. This search engine uses tools freely available on the Web to gather environmental science related information on the Web.

Web mining, which emerged in the late 1990s, is a cross-disciplinary field. This book is an effort to bridge the gap between information search and data mining on the Web. The book provides enough background information on both fields by presenting the intuition and mechanics of the best tools in each field, as well as how they work together. We hope that this book will encourage people with different backgrounds to contribute to Web mining.

The book is targeted towards researchers and developers of Web information systems. It can serve as a supplemental text book to a one-semester undergraduate/graduate course on data mining, databases and information retrieval.

Acknowledgments

We would like to express our sincere gratitude to all those who have worked with us in all aspects related to this book. Those include Francine Abeles, Jeff Cheng, Eunice W. Healey, Stanley H. Lipson, Amit Revankar, Gunjan Samtani, and Jeanie Hsiang for the cover design. We also wish to thank Bruce Croft, Series Editor of the Information Retrieval series, Scott Delman, Senior Publishing Editor, and Melissa Fearon, Editorial Assistant of Kluwer Academic Publishers, for their guiding us through the materialization and publication of this book. G. Chang's work was partially supported by Kean University's Un-tenured Faculty Research Grants. J. McHugh's work was supported by New Jersey Information-Technology Opportunities for the Workforce, Education, and Research (NJ I-TOWER) grant, a project funded by the NJ Commission on Higher Education (contract #: 01-801020-02).

I
INFORMATION RETRIEVAL ON THE WEB

Chapter 1

KEYWORD-BASED SEARCH ENGINES

The World Wide Web (WWW), also known as the Web, was introduced in 1992 at the Center for European Nuclear Research (CERN) in Switzerland [28]. What began as a means of facilitating data sharing in different formats among physicists at CERN is today a mammoth, heterogeneous, non-administered, distributed, global information system that is revolutionizing the information age. The Web is organized as a set of hypertext documents interconnected by hyperlinks, used in the *Hypertext Markup Language* (HTML) to construct links between documents. The many potential benefits the Web augurs have spurred research in information search/filtering [54, 154], Web/database integration [43, 168], Web querying systems [3, 150, 155, 187], and data mining [66, 252]. The Web has also brought together researchers from areas as diverse as communications, electronic publishing, language processing, and databases, as well as from multiple scientific and business domains.

Prior to the Web, the Internet was only a massive interconnected network of computers, which was text oriented and used primarily by large corporations and research institutes for sharing information. Since the inception of the Web, the Internet has experienced explosive growth both in the number of users and the amount of content available on it. The Web has added the interconnection between documents with different contents. The contents include images, graphics, sound and video, in addition to text. Millions of knowledgeable Internet users have turned the Web into a remarkable repository of information. Indeed, the ability of the Web to collect and to disseminate information has in a few short years arguably transcended what television broadcasting took 50 years to accomplish.

The availability of user-friendly, graphics-oriented interfaces has contributed substantially to the growth and usefulness of the Web . Browsers, such as Netscape Navigator and Internet Explorer, and multimedia players such as RealPlayer, have greatly simplified the use of the Internet and expanded its appeal. However, the Web's rapid growth has exacerbated the burden of sifting and winnowing the information that can be accessed on the Web. In many respects, the Web is similar to a library with a limited catalog system: full of valuable information, but confusing and time-consuming to search.

As the number of computers connected to the Internet grows, so does the volume of content on the Web. Ironically, the same hyperlink organization that gives the Web its power, also makes its organization remarkably chaotic. Searching for specific information has become increasingly difficult in this dynamic, distributed, heterogeneous, and unstructured repository. Using browsing as a search method is often a problematic option for finding wanted information, frequently like looking for a needle in a haystack. These challenges, however, have led to many important developments.

This book concentrates on four of these developments:

- *Keyword-Based Search Engines*

- *Query-Based Search Systems*

- *Mediators and Wrappers*

- *Multimedia Search Engines*

In this chapter, we focus on keyword-based search engines and related techniques. Chapter 2 addresses issues in query based search. Chapter 3 discusses mediators and wrappers. Chapter 4 describes multimedia search engines. The techniques presented are not all new to the information retrieval and database community. Rather, the emergence of the Web has promoted the refinement and perfection of existing techniques in hardware and software to meet the demands of the Internet.

1.   SEARCH ENGINES

Web search engines, also called *Web indexes*, *index servers*, or simply *search engines*, have become the most visited Web sites on the Internet. Indeed, the most common method used today to search the Web consists of sending information requests to these servers, which index as many documents as they can find by navigating the Web. A salient problem is that an informed user must be aware of the various index servers, their strengths, weaknesses, and the peculiarities of their query interfaces. The need for querying information on the Web has led to the development of a number of tools that search these indexes based on keywords specified by users.

Several such tools, e.g., AltaVista [13] and WebCrawler [264], have become the gateway to the Web for the neophyte and information oracles for the experienced. These tools serve the information needs of users by finding useful information in the sea of Internet data. While early search engines were research prototypes, today's search engines represent billions of dollars of invested capital. They are maintained by commercial firms to promote services primarily related to e-commerce.

Search engines are similar to ordinary library search systems in that they allow users to type in subjects of interest as keywords, and return a set of results satisfying given conditions. However, search engines seek, update, and index documents on a far more massive scale than library systems. In addition, the Web is a far more dynamic domain than a library, making it harder to maintain the currency of indexes.

According to a recent survey [125], the most popular search engines include AltaVista [13], Excite [89] (Magellan and WebCrawler have been acquired by Excite), HotBot [133], Infoseek [109], Lycos [172], Yahoo! [275]. These search engines are multi-domain oriented and span the entire Web. AltaVista acts like the Yellow Pages for the Web. It indexes the full-text of documents. Excite uses artificial intelligence, employing concept-driven or "fuzzy" search. HotBot's Slurp spider is the most powerful of all the Web "crawlers", capable of indexing the entire Web in about a week, an ability which translates into fewer out-of-date links. Infoseek is the most user-friendly search engine, with a clean, intuitive interface. Lycos is like a bibliographic database service except that its abstracts are generated by programs called Web crawlers, rather than human indexers. Yahoo! is actually not a search engine, but rather a directory of the Web compiled manually by human indexers. Some search engines focus on single domains [107]. Others are meta-search ones that harness the power of multiple existing search engines. Still others employ user profiles known, in Web parlance, as "cookies", and server logs to determine the most popular sites.

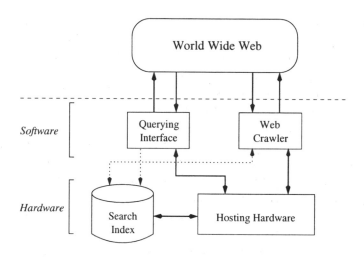

Figure 1.1.   The architecture of a search engine.

Another very popular search engine, Google [114], has recently announced that its searches encompass an average of more than one billion (10^9) pages. Its index consists of 560 million full-text and 500 million partially indexed pages. This news has placed Google as the largest index on the Internet.

Search Engine Watch [234], a portal on search engine news and resources, categorizes search engines as: *Major, Kids, Meta, Multimedia, News, Regional,* and *Specialized.* Typically, a search engine has four major components: *Querying Interface, Search Index, Web Crawler,* and *Hosting Hardware,* as illustrated in Figure 1.1. The solid lines in this figure represent direct interactions; dotted lines are indirect interactions between components. We describe the first three components in detail below. Hardware issues are beyond the scope of this book. We direct the reader to [222] for a discussion of the hardware that powers the AltaVista search engine as an illustration of the hardware environments.

1.1   QUERYING INTERFACE

The querying interface is the software component that searches indexes to find matches based on search criteria provided in a *query.* Retrieved documents are ranked according to a predefined relevance matrix. In a keyword-based query, combinations of keywords can be formulated to search for documents

Field	Field Location	Example
text:	Body	text:information
title:	Title	title:database
link:	Hyperlink	link:kluwer.nl
anchor:	Visual Part of a Hyperlink	anchor:mining
url:	URL	url:www.xyz.com
host:	Computer Name	host:xyz.com
domain:	Specific Domain	domain:edu
image:	Image Name	image:map.gif
applet:	Applet Name	applet:tetris
object:	Object Name	object:game

Table 1.1.   Searchable Web page fields.

containing such keywords. Such an interface is simple, intuitive, and easy to use, even for naive users. Its more effective use requires experience and more complex combinations of keywords and operators.

In this subsection, we discuss some of the most popular ways of formulating keyword-based queries for search engines.

1.1.1   SINGLE-WORD QUERY

This is the most elementary querying interface for a search engine. In this model, a keyword is used as an input to the search engine. The result of the search is the set of documents containing at least one occurrence of the input keyword. Depending on the model used by the search engine index, the keyword could occur as a word or as part of a word in the document. A semantically enhanced version of keyword search, called *field* search, is provided by some systems to focus the search on specific structural aspects of a Web page. For example, a query with the term, `title:"information"`, would return only documents with `information` in the title, using the HTML tags of a document to identify document components such as titles. Table 1.1 summarizes a list of commonly used search fields.

1.1.2   MULTIPLE-TERM QUERY

In this model, the querying keyword is not restricted to a single word or phrase. Multiple terms can be used in formulating query criteria. The terms can be basic terms (words) or Boolean expressions built on the basic terms. Most search engines minimally provide the following user-selected methods of expressing multiple-term queries:

- Resulting documents must contain *all* the keywords.

- Resulting documents must contain *any* of the keywords.

For example, a multiple-term query such as "information and database" is used to find all documents containing both of the words "information" and "database". A query with expressions such as "((data or Web) and mining)" identifies all documents containing either "data and mining" or "Web and mining". In general, one can use Boolean operators as connectives to connect two terms. Let e_1 and e_2 be two terms. The most commonly used Boolean operators are:

- and – for combining query terms. For example, the query (e_1 and e_2) selects all documents that contain both e_1 and e_2.

- or – for including either the first or the second term. For example, the query (e_1 or e_2) selects all documents that contain e_1 or e_2.

- not – for excluding documents with a query term. For example, the query (not e_1) excludes documents with e_1 from the result.

Clearly, these three operators can only be performed on documents indexed by a search engine. Duplicates are removed from the result.

1.1.3   CONTEXT BASED QUERY

When the context of the querying keyword is known, a query can be formulated using phrase and proximity querying. These two methods can improve the search efforts by eliminating documents that do not satisfy this stricter form of multiple-term query.

A phrase is defined as any set of words that appear in a specific order. We note that in a multiple-term query, the order of the querying keywords is not important because search engines evaluate each keyword individually. In contrast, in a phrase search, the order of the querying keywords is important. Typically, querying phrases are enclosed inside quotation marks (" "). They can be used to search for particular sentences, for example, "I have a dream."

In proximity querying, the user can specify a sequence of terms (words or phrases) and a maximum allowed *distance* between any two terms. This distance can be measured in characters or words, depending on the index. For example, the AltaVista search engine uses an adjacency operator near to denote the textual closeness of two terms. The retrieved documents must contain the two terms, which must be within ten words of each other. Proximity querying is helpful in, for example, searching for names because first and last names may be separated by middle names and initials. In general, near is useful when the proximity between two words reflects or captures some semantic connection.

1.1.4   NATURAL LANGUAGE QUERY

A major problem search services face is the complexity of the querying interface, which is often too complicated for naive users. Formulating a Boolean query is difficult and frustrating for many people. As a result, systems such as AskJeeves [19] and ElectricMonk [85] have developed natural language interfaces. These services do an impressive job of getting people to find what they want by prompting users to form their own questions. Questions like: "Where can I find a digital camera?" and "Which models of cars are most popular?" can be posed and very accurate responses provided.

The secret to the accuracy of AskJeeves is human intervention. A team of developers creates the knowledge base of questions that powers the search engine. Currently, there are more than seven million questions in the AskJeeves knowledge base. Popular questions that are very frequently asked have prebuilt answers targeted for those questions including lists of subsequent questions useful to narrow the search. If AskJeeves cannot find a match of the asked question in its knowledge base of questions, it falls back on its meta-search engine component to retrieve various search engine results as a backup.

Natural language query is the trend of future information retrieval systems since it is more intuitive for casual users to formulate search criteria in natural language. Strictly speaking, search engines with such a capability should not be categorized as keyword-based ones; instead they should be considered as natural language search engines.

1.1.5   PATTERN MATCHING QUERY

In a pattern matching query, the objective is to retrieve all documents that match a given pattern. In this case, it is often difficult to rank results because the given pattern might not contain exact words.

Search engines like AltaVista provide a way to broaden a search by using *wildcards*. Wildcards are simply placeholders for missing characters. The main idea is to allow the missing characters, represented by an asterisk (*), to match an arbitrary character(s),   in order to increase the number of related hits. For example, colo*r will match both *color*, the American spelling, and *colour*, the British spelling.

Restrictions are placed on wildcards because they can broaden a search excessively. AltaVista implements the following two guidelines on wildcards usage:

- Use wildcards only after three or more characters.

- Use wildcards as placeholders for up to 5 unknown characters.

Some systems allow searching using regular expressions [132]. Enhanced regular expressions [274] extend the expressive power of regular expressions. They incorporate constructs like character class, conditional expression, wildcards, and exact and approximate matching operations to make patterns more powerful.

One definition of approximate matching is based on the concept of edit distance. Given two strings S_1 and S_2 the *edit distance* between S_1 and S_2 is defined as the minimum number of *edit operations* (*delete*, *insert* and *relabel*) needed to transform one to the other as illustrated in Figure 1.2. In this figure, three edit operations are required to transform S_1 to S_2 (via relabeling V to U, deleting M, and inserting L). Algorithms for finding the edit distance between two strings can be found in [237]. Approximate text matching over hypertext, on the Web, can be found in [14, 203, 274].

Figure 1.2.   String edit operations.

Since matching regular and extended regular expressions is computationally expensive, it is not implemented on a large scale for the Web and is not

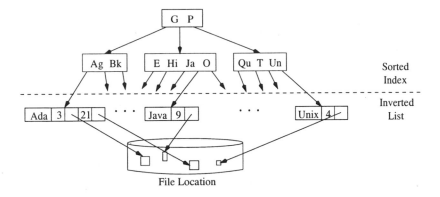

Figure 1.3.   An inverted file built based on a B-tree.

widely adopted by major search engines. However, approximate matching is implemented in WebGlimpse [177], which is based on Glimpse [178].

1.2   SEARCH INDEX

The *search index*, or simply *index*, is the heart of a search engine. The index is typically a list of keywords; each keyword is associated with a list of corresponding documents that contain the keyword. In order to provide fast response time for thousands of concurrent users and be able to store large volumes of data, most search engines use inverted file indexing.

The search index is used because sequential string search algorithms [10, 37, 144, 149] are impractical when the text collection is large, especially if searching is a very frequently performed operation, as it is in systems such as database servers and library information systems. The most widely used method to speed up text search is to prebuild an index. Building and maintaining an index when the amount of text is large and dynamic is not an easy task. Therefore, various indexing techniques, including inverted files [18], suffix arrays [113, 176], suffix trees [10, 184, 258] and signature files [90, 91], have been developed and studied. Most search engines use inverted files because they are easier to maintain and to implement.

An inverted file is an enormous, word-oriented, look-up table. It contains two major parts: a *sorted index* (list) of keywords (vocabulary) and an *inverted list* that stores a list of pointers to all occurrences of a keyword as illustrated in Figure 1.3. In this figure, the internal nodes represent the index structure,

Type	Space Requirement	Access Speed	Accuracy
coarse-grained	low	low	low
medium-grained	medium	medium	high
fine-grained	very high	very fast	exact

Table 1.2.   Granularity of inverted file indexes.

while the leaf nodes contain the indexed words with their occurrence position within the file and pointers to different file locations. In the case in which the inverted index is used for the Web, the locations referred to are URLs. Inverted files can be implemented using a variety of data structures. The sorted index (list) can be built using sorted arrays, hash tables, B-trees [24, 25], tries [38], or a combination of these.

Different search engines use different inverted file indexing schemes. The *granularity* of an index is defined as the accuracy to which the index identifies the location of a search keyword. In general, indexes can be classified into the following three categories:

- *Coarse-grained* – able to identify a set of documents based on a search keyword.

- *Medium-grained* – able to identify a specific document based on a search keyword.

- *Fine-grained* – able to identify a sentence or word location in a specific document based on a search keyword.

Each granularity classification has different storage requirements and precision, as summarized in Table 1.2.

In the case of Web search engines, instead of storing the locations of keyword occurrences, the search index stores the URLs of the occurrences, as illustrated in Figure 1.4. The triangular shape in Figure 1.4 represents a B-tree index. The listing of URLs indexed by the B-tree is shown in a table on the right of the figure. Each posting list refers to a list of pointers to those URLs where a particular keyword occurs, with one posting list per keyword. The order of the URLs in a posting list for a keyword depends on an internal ranking mechanism

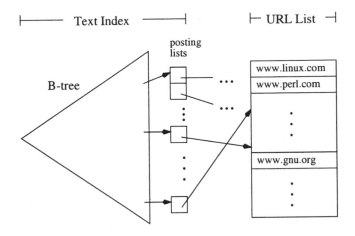

Figure 1.4.   Index structure of a Web search engine.

based on criteria such as word frequency count and word weight, which are used to measure the importance of a word within a document.

The Web has become a global information resource, with obvious consequences for the size of the index. In order to reduce the size of the index, the following kinds of transformation techniques are used in the index building process. Index compression techniques are also applied to represent indexes more compactly.

- *Case folding* – converts everything to lower case. For example, Data Mining becomes data mining.

- *Stemming* – reduces words to their morphological root. For example, compression and compressed become compress.

- *Stop word removal* – removes common or semantically insignificant words. For example, the definite article, the, and indefinite articles, a and an in English, are removed.

- *Text compression* – reduces the inverted file size.

Different search engines apply the transformation methods differently. The methods are *domain* and *language* specific. For example, "SAT" and "Sat", and "US" and "us" have different meanings in English. Therefore, modifications to these methods are made to reflect different domains and languages. More detailed information on document compressing and indexing is discussed in [272].

1.3   WEB CRAWLERS

Web crawlers, also known as *agents*, *robots* or *spiders*, are programs that work continuously behind the scene, having the essential role of locating information on the Web and retrieving it for indexing.

Crawlers run continuously to ensure an index is kept as up to date as possible and to achieve the broadest possible coverage of the Web. However, since the Web is constantly changing and expanding, no search engine can feasibly cover the whole Web. Indeed, many studies that have been conducted to estimate the coverage of search engines employing crawlers, show that coverage ranges between only 5% to 30% [162] and the union of 11 major search engines covers less than 50% of the Web [163].

Claiming broader coverage of the Web is one way of demonstrating the superiority of an index. Search engine firms tend to use the extent of their coverage to boast about their indexing technology. However, broader coverage does not by itself guarantee higher accuracy. Most search engines attempt to maximize *recall*, a figure of merit used in information retrieval, defined as:

$$recall = \frac{N}{T},$$

where N denotes the number of retrieved documents that are relevant to a search query and T denotes the number of potentially retrievable Web documents that are relevant to the search query. Observe that this is not the ratio of retrieved to relevant documents, which could be considerably greater than 100% since a large number of irrelevant documents could be included in what are retrieved.

Another measure of the effectiveness of search engines is *precision*, defined as:

$$precision = \frac{N}{R},$$

where R denotes the number of documents retrieved in response to the search query. Low precision would indicate that many irrelevant or superfluous documents are retrieved, while low recall would indicate that the fraction of potentially relevant documents retrieved is low. Thus, recall and precision tend to be

- Arts & Humanities
- Business & Economy
- Computer & Internet
- Education
- Entertainment
- Government
- Health

- News & Media
- Recreation & Sports
- Reference
- Regional
- Science
- Social Science
- Society & Culture

Table 1.3.   Yahoo! directory categories.

inversely related: when recall is high, precision tends to be low, as illustrated in Figure 1.5.

Although there are many publicly available search engines, the details of how specific indexes are organized remain a strategic business secret. The in-depth coverage on crawlers will be discussed in Chapter 8.

2.   WEB DIRECTORIES

Search engines such as Northern Light [208], Direct Hit [79], Inktomi [136], FAST Search [93], create their index automatically using crawlers. On the other hand, Yahoo! [275] depends on humans to create its listing, called a *directory*. Directories are created by using Website descriptions submitted by various sites or generated by human editors. Table 1.3 illustrates directory categories listed

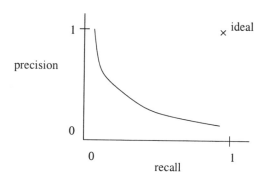

Figure 1.5.   Recall-precision curve.

on Yahoo! directory main page. Similar category structures can be found at other search engines, like Excite [89], Netscape [205], and Go [109].

Although directories and indexes work differently on the backend, the querying interface frontends work similarly.

3.   META-SEARCH ENGINES

Search engines provide fast retrieval of information of interest from the Web. However, the problem of knowing where search engines are and how to use them poses some difficulties. Furthermore, empirical results indicate that only 45% of relevant results will likely be returned by a single search engine [235], that is, each has a recall rate of 45%. This limitation is compounded by the fact that the coverage of a typical search engine is between only 5% – 30% of the Web [162].

Meta-search engines are designed to mitigate such problems by accessing multiple individual search engines. The principle behind meta-search engines like MetaCrawler [189], SherlockHound [241], SavvySearch [231], and Inquirus [161], is simple: "A dozen search engines is better than one". The system architecture of MetaCrawler is discussed in [81, 236] and an improved meta-search architecture has been presented and studied in [108]. Figure 1.6 illustrates the system architecture of a meta-search engine that contains the following components:

- Query Interface Module – responsible for getting user's query input.

- Dispatch Module – responsible for determining to which search engines a specific query is sent.

- Knowledge-base Module – used by the Dispatch Module to perform decision-making (optional).

- Interface Agents Module – responsible for interacting with different search engines using different query formats.

- Evaluation Module – responsible for ranking results according to some predefined evaluation methods (optional).

- Display Module – responsible for displaying results.

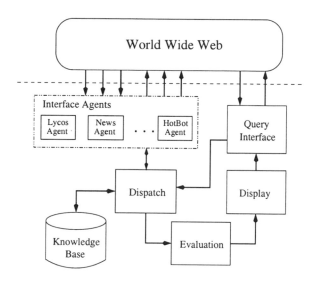

Figure 1.6.   The architecture of a meta-search engine.

4.   INFORMATION FILTERING

An important tool which is complementary to the search engine approach is information filtering [23]. Filtering refers to the process of determining whether a document is relevant to search criteria or not, and eliminating irrelevant documents. Filtering applications usually involve a stream of incoming data such as newswire and email. Filtering is also used to describe the process of accessing and searching for information on remote servers using intelligent agents [26].

Information filtering, which is based on a combination of machine learning and information retrieval techniques [54, 69, 70, 103, 157, 183, 207, 232], has been employed in many specialized search engines. Information filters can be viewed as mediators between information sources and target systems. They help systems eliminate irrelevant information using intelligent decision-making techniques like Bayesian classifiers, term-frequency analysis, k-neighbors, neural networks, rule-learning, etc.

Information filtering tools can be used to build topic-specific search engines. General-purpose search engines, such as HotBot [133], offer high levels of Web coverage for general information search on the Web. However, topic-specific

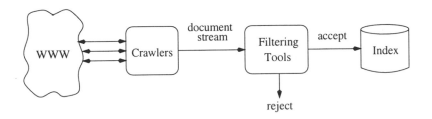

Figure 1.7.   The building process of a topic-specific search engine.

search engines are growing in popularity because they offer an increased precision/recall rate. Examples of topic-specific search engines are: DejaNews [75], which specializes in Usenet news articles; BioCrawler [35], which is a directory and search engine for biological information search; and Cora [68], which allows one to search for computer science research papers in PostScript format from universities and labs all over the world.

A general process for building a topic-specific search engine is illustrated in Figure 1.7. In this figure, the agents which are responsible for retrieving documents from the Web are crawlers. Documents returned by crawlers are streamed to information filtering tools, which decide the relevance of the documents to the topic domain. Accepted documents are added to the search index, while rejected documents are discarded.

Chapter 2

QUERY-BASED SEARCH SYSTEMS

A shortcoming of the keyword-based search tools discussed in Chapter 1 is the lack of high-level querying facilities available to facilitate information retrieval on the Web. Query languages have long been part of database management systems (DBMSs), the standard DBMS query language being the Structural Query Language (SQL) [104, 151, 221]. Such query languages not only provide a structural way of accessing the data stored in a database, but also hide details of the database structure from the user. Since the Web is often viewed as a gigantic database holding vast stores of information, some Web-oriented query systems have been developed. However, unlike the highly structured data found in a DBMS, information on the Web is stored mainly as files. The files can be generally categorized as:

- *Structured*, such as flat databases and BibTeX files.

- *Semistructured*, such as HTML, XML, and LaTeX files.

- *Unstructured*, such as sound, image, pure text and executable files.

Structured files have a strict inner structure. For example, files like BibTeX are highly structured. The grammar of BibTeX precisely defines the syntax and semantics of the data. In this case, the grammar is like the schema of a database.

Semistructured files are text files that contain formatting codes, often called *tags*. Such files include LaTeX, HTML, and XML files. Although tags can be used to specify the semantic information within documents, most of the semantic information is not coded in a formal way. Furthermore, even if the semantics were formally coded, they would not be at a fine-grained level of specification like in a database schema. For example, the \paragraph tag in LaTeX and the <P> tag in HTML documents are general tags but say nothing about the content of a paragraph. XML provides a finer grained specification than HTML by allowing user-defined tags, but the lack of data type support and querying facilities has led to the further development of XML-data [164], XML-QL [76, 99], and the Niagara Internet Query System (NiagaraCQ) [57].

Unstructured files include sound, image and executable files that are not text based. This makes it difficult to apply database techniques such as querying and indexing to them.

Web query languages that have been developed and that allow high-level querying facility on the Web include W3QS/W3QL [150], WebSQL [187], WAQL [125], and WebLog [155]. These systems allow the user to pose SQL-like queries on the Web, with the exception of WebLog which uses a logic-like query format. Unlike the query facilities provided in mediators to be described in Chapter 3, these query systems interact directly with the Web with minimal interaction with a local DBMS or a file system. The general architecture of these query systems is illustrated in Figure 2.1. It consists of a **Query Parser** module, a **Query Engine** module, and system utilities. **Query Parser** takes a query and sends it to **Query Engine**. **Query Engine** interacts with search engines, Web servers, system utilities and file systems. We will discuss W3QS/W3QL, WebSQL and WAQL in this chapter, and refer the reader to the reference [155] for a discussion of WebLog.

1.   W3QS/W3QL

W3QS [150] was one of the first Web querying systems. The system was designed to provide:

- a high-level SQL-like query language,

- a simple interface to external programs and Unix tools,

- a graphical user interface for the information gathered by queries, and

- a higher view maintenance facility than robot-maintained indexes.

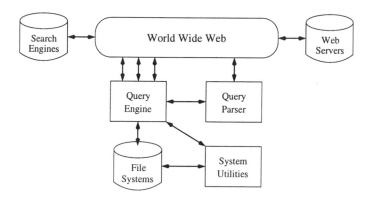

Figure 2.1.   Web querying system architecture.

A query language called W3QL was subsequently designed as part of the W3QS system. W3QL is an SQL-like language that allows querying based on the organization and HTML content of the hypertext. It emphasizes extensibility and the ability to interact with user-written programs, Unix utilities, and tools for managing Web forms. Its ability to interact with external programs makes W3QL like a command-driven query language.

W3QL views the Web as a directed graph. Each URL or document corresponds to a node of the graph. Each node has associated properties according to its document type and content. For example, a node corresponding to an HTML file has an HTML format, a URL, a Title, etc. On the other hand, a node corresponding to a LATEX file is of LATEX format and might have Author and Title associated with it. A directed edge is drawn from node a to node b if node a is a node with HTML or XML format and the document contains at least one anchor (hyperlink) to node b. Like nodes, edges also have associated properties. For example, consider Figure 2.2 which illustrates a structure-based path pattern query. This query is to find documents with "airplane" in their title and with a hyperlink to Boeing's Website with an image on 747. The <A> tag which specifies the hyperlink corresponds to a directed edge with attributes such as HREF and REV. Since there may be more than one hyperlink between a pair of nodes, the Web actually corresponds to a labelled directed multigraph.

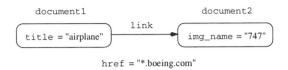

Figure 2.2.   Structure-based query.

W3QL provides two types of hypertext query: *content*-based and *structure*-based.   In content-based queries, W3QL uses a program called SQLCOND to evaluate Boolean expressions in the query. This is similar to the WHERE clause of an SQL query. Using SQLCOND, a user can select nodes from the Web that satisfy certain conditions. For example, the conditions might be:

    (node.format = HTML) and (node.title = "database").

In a structure-based query, the query can be specified using a *path pattern* (*path expression*).   A *path* is a set of nodes $\{n_1,\ldots,n_k\}$, and node pairs (n_i, n_{i+1}), $1 \leq i \leq k - 1$, where (n_i, n_{i+1}) are edges of the graph.

The query patterns are a set of subgraphs of the Web in graph representation. Each subgraph must satisfy conditions in the query pattern including node and edge conditions specified by the query pattern.

W3QS/W3QL has three main modules - a **Query Processor**, a **Remote Search Program** (RSP), and a **Format Library**. The **Query Processor** takes a query and invokes programs in the RSP library to interact with search engines. At the end of the search, the **Format Library** is used to display the result.

The semantics of a W3QL query is defined as follows:

SELECT	α
FROM	β
WHERE	ω
USING	ψ
EVALUATED EVERY	γ

where α specifies how results should be processed; β specifies the pattern graph of the search domain; ω specifies a set of conditions on the nodes and edges specified in β; ψ and γ optionally specify the search methods and search interval, respectively.

1.1 SELECT CLAUSE

The SELECT clause is an optional part of the query and defines the form in which the query results should be processed. It has the following form:

$$\text{SELECT [CONTINUOUSLY] statements.} \qquad (2.1)$$

The statements are UNIX programs and arguments that are invoked after the results are returned from the RSP. This clause may also involve running a UNIX program to process the result. It can also act as a filter to reformat the result.

1.2 FROM CLAUSE

The FROM clause describes the virtual pattern graph the RSP uses to search for results. Patterns are described using a set of paths according to the following format:

$$\text{FROM path\_expressions.} \qquad (2.2)$$

The path_expressions specify the search pattern to be used by the RSP. A pattern graph is a directed graph $G(V, E)$ where there is at most one edge between any two nodes and at most one self-loop. Figure 2.3 illustrates a pattern graph with its corresponding text description.

1.3 WHERE CLAUSE

The WHERE clause is used to specify search predicates that nodes and edges in the FROM clause must satisfy. Only nodes satisfying the WHERE conditions will be returned as part of the query results. The WHERE clause has the following form:

$$\text{WHERE condition\_clauses.} \qquad (2.3)$$

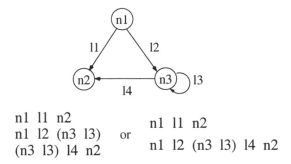

nl ll n2
nl l2 (n3 l3)   or   nl ll n2
(n3 l3) l4 n2   nl l2 (n3 l3) l4 n2

Figure 2.3.   Example of a pattern graph.

The condition_clauses impose search restrictions on the nodes and edges specified in the FROM clause. It can also provide RSP navigation directives. The following are conditions that can be specified:

- unix_program args = reg_expression.   This will invoke external UNIX programs.

- node_name IN file_name.   This will check whether the node name node_name is in the file file_name.

- FILL node_name AS IN file_name WITH assignments. This will automatically fill in the form in node_name with data found in file_name and assignments.

- RUN unix_program IF node_name UNKNOWN IN file_name. This will automatically invoke an external program if an unknown form is encountered during the search process.

1.4   USING CLAUSE

The USING clause is optionally used to specify the search algorithm to be performed by the RSP. Search methods like depth first search and breadth first search can be specified. If the algorithm is not specified in a query, a default search algorithm is used.

1.5   EVALUATED EVERY CLAUSE

The EVALUATED EVERY clause is optionally used to specify the updating interval for the query. Intervals such as daily and weekly can be specified for automatic updates. This clause is mainly used for dynamically maintained views.

1.6   EXAMPLES

Example 1. This query searches for HTML documents that contain hyperlinks to images in GIF format located in www.xyz.com. Here n1 and n2 are nodes and l1 is the link used to connect n1 with n2. The select statement is a command that copies the content of n1 to a file called result.

```
select   cp n1/* result;
from     n1, l1, n2;
where    SQLCOND (n1.format = HTML) AND
         (l1.href = "www.xyz.com") AND
         (n2.name = "*.gif");
```

Example 2. This query defines a view which maintains a list of pointers to LaTeX articles with "Data Mining" in the title. URLlist.url specifies a built-in list of important search indexes. URLlist.fil specifies how to fill in the keyword "Data Mining" in HTML forms required by search indexes in URLlist.url. The select statement specifies that the URL of n2 should be printed continuously.

```
select   CONTINUOUSLY SQLPRINT n2.URL;
from     n1, l1, n2;
where    n1 IN URLlist.url;
         FILL n1.form AS IN URLlist.fil WITH keyword="Data Mining";
         SQLCOND (n2.format = "LaTeX") AND
         (n2.title = "Data Mining");
```

2.   WEBSQL

WebSQL [187] is another SQL-like query language in the spirit of W3QL which represents an effort towards greater formalization. It introduces some interesting ideas including:

- a high-level SQL-like query language,

- a querying interface implemented in Java,

- a new theory of query cost based on "query locality,"

- the ability to use multiple index servers without explicit user knowledge, and

- the ability for Web maintenance.

WebSQL is also based on a graph model of a document network. It views the Web as a "virtual graph" whose nodes are documents and whose directed edges are hyperlinks. To find a document in this graph, one navigates starting from known nodes or with the assistance of index servers. Given a URL u, an agent can be used to fetch all nodes reachable from u by examining anchors in the document contents. Conversely, nodes that have links to u can be found by querying index servers for nodes that contain links to node u, using `link:url` search format in the AltaVista [13] search engine.

The semantics of a WebSQL query is defined using, for example, selections and projections. A query has the form:

```
SELECT   α
FROM     β
WHERE    ω
```

where α specifies attributes of documents that satisfy a given predicate; β specifies the domain conditions of the attributes; and ω specifies a set of Boolean expressions that a query must satisfy.

2.1   SELECT CLAUSE

The SELECT clause is used to list the attributes desired for the result of a query. It has the form:

$$\texttt{SELECT Ident.} attrib_1, \ \ldots, \texttt{Ident.} attrib_n, \tag{2.4}$$

where `Ident.`$attrib_i$ are identifer and attribute pairs. The attributes can be any combination of the following:

- `url` – for retrieving the Uniform Resource Locator.

- `title` – for retrieving the title of the document.

- `text` – for retrieving the actual hypertext.

- `type` – for retrieving specific document format.

- `length` – for retrieving the length of a document.

- `modif` – for retrieving the last modification date.

2.2 FROM CLAUSE

The `FROM` clause is used to list the domain conditions for the attributes desired for the result of a query. It has the following form:

$$\texttt{FROM DocType Ident SUCH THAT DomainCondition,} \tag{2.5}$$

where `DocType` specifies the document or structure type such as *document, anchor, sound, image*; `Ident` is a tuple variable; and `DomainCondition` specifies the condition of the domain based on the following forms:

- Node *PathRegExp* TableVariable

- TableVariable MENTIONS StringConstant

- Attribute = Node

PathRegExp is used to specify a path regular expression based on hyperlink structures, where a hyperlink can be one of the following types:

- *Interior* – if its target is within the source document;

- *Local* – if its target is a different document on the same server;

- *Global* – if its target is located on a different server.

Arrow-like symbols are used to denote the three link types; thus, $\mapsto$ denotes an interior link, $\rightarrow$ denotes a local link, and $\Rightarrow$ denotes a global link. In addition, = denotes the empty path. Using these three link types, one can build path regular expressions using concatenation, alternation (|) and repetition (*).

2.3   WHERE CLAUSE

The WHERE clause is used to specify search predicates that documents returned from the FROM clause must satisfy. Only documents satisfying the WHERE conditions will be returned as part of the query results. It has the following form:

$$\text{WHERE } Term_1 \; \mathcal{LC} \; \ldots \; \mathcal{LC} \; Term_n. \tag{2.6}$$

The search predicates are Boolean expressions consisting of terms connected by logical connectives ($\mathcal{LC}$), with *and* denoting intersection and *or* denoting union.

2.4   EXAMPLES

Example 1. This query is used to search for HTML documents about "mining". It returns the URL of the documents in the tuple d.

```
select    d.url
from      Document d
          SUCH THAT d MENTIONS "mining"
where     d.type = "text/html";
```

Example 2. This query is used to search for documents about "mining" that contain a hyperlink to www.kdd.org. It returns the URL and title of the documents in the tuple d.

```
select    d.url, d.title
from      Document d
          SUCH THAT d MENTIONS "mining",
          Anchor y SUCH THAT base = d
where     y.href = "www.kdd.org";
```

Example 3. This query is used to search for documents with "Web mining" in the title, which are linked from a hyperlink path originating at www.kdd.org, of length two or less, and located on the local server. It returns the URL and title of the documents in the tuple d.

```
select   d.url, d.title
from     Document d
         SUCH THAT "http://www.kdd.org" = | → | → → d
where    d.title = "Web mining";
```

3. WAQL

WAQL [125] (Web-based Approximate Query Language) is an SQL-like language similar to W3QL and WebSQL. It can interact with both search engines and Websites and automate the search/gathering process. It acts like an agent that controls the information searching process according to the user's specification. It was designed to provide:

- a high-level SQL-like query language,

- a structural search mechanism based on document structure,

- approximate search based on edit distance, and

- approximate search based on variable length don't cares.

The semantics of a WAQL query has the form:

$$
\begin{array}{ll}
\text{SELECT} & \alpha \\
\text{FROM} & \beta \\
\text{USING} & \gamma \\
\text{WHERE} & \omega
\end{array}
$$

where α specifies attributes of documents that satisfy a given predicate; β specifies which Website to search; γ specifies which index servers should be used; and ω specifies a set of Boolean expressions that a query result must satisfy.

3.1 SELECT CLAUSE

The SELECT clause is used to list the attributes desired as the result of a query. It has the following form:

$$\text{SELECT Ident.}attrib_1,\ \ldots,\text{Ident.}attrib_n, \qquad (2.7)$$

where Ident.$attrib_i$ are identifer and attribute pairs. The attributes can be any combination of the following:

- url – for retrieving the Uniform Resource Locator.

- title – for retrieving the title of the document.

- size – for retrieving the size of the document.

- text – for retrieving the actual hypertext.

- modif – for retrieving the last modification date.

- dist – for specifying the distance between query and actual document.

3.2   FROM CLAUSE

The FROM clause is used to specify which Website to contact and retrieve documents from. It has the following form:

$$\text{FROM URL }\{,\text{URL}\}\text{ Ident traversal\_method [target\_range]}. \quad (2.8)$$

The FROM clause is used to perform a site-oriented search that traverses the entire Website. The URL field specifies the address of a target site. The Ident field is a pointer to each document returned by the traversal. Let I_1 and I_n denote integer type. When the target_range field has the form I_n, it informs the query processor to process the 1st to the I_nth URL; when it has the form $I_1..I_n$, it informs the query processor to process the I_1th to the I_nth URL.

When performing a Website oriented search, hyperlinks (URLs) encountered within hypertext documents during the navigation are of the following types:

- *Local-links*, which are hyperlinks that link to the same domain.

- *External-links*, which are hyperlinks that link to different domains.

- *All-links*, which include both local and external links.

Operator	Definition of Operator
− >	Breadth first traversal only on local-link.
=>	Breadth first traversal only on external-link.
+ >	Breadth first traversal on all-links.
| >	Depth first traversal only on local-link.
|| >	Depth first traversal only on external-link.
||| >	Depth first traversal on all-links.

Table 2.1.   Operators specifying the traversal method on a specific link type.

The traversal methods, which can be performed using any specified combinations of these different hyperlink types, are:

- *Depth first* – Documents are retrieved in the depth first search order with respect to the hyperlinks.

- *Breadth first* – Documents are retrieved in the breadth first search order with respect to the hyperlinks.

Table 2.1 shows a list of operators that specify hyperlink types and their respective traversal methods.

3.3   USING CLAUSE

The USING clause is used to specify which index server to contact for an initial search. It has the following form:

$$\text{USING search\_engine Ident [target\_range]}. \qquad (2.9)$$

The search_engine field specifies which index server to request for the target documents. WAQL provides interfaces to five publicly available search engines: AltaVista, Excite, Hotbot, Infoseek, and Lycos.

Ident is a tuple variable that acts like a pointer to each document returned by the search engines. The target_range field has the same interpretation as for the FROM clause.

3.4   WHERE CLAUSE

The WHERE clause is used to specify search predicates that documents returned from the FROM clause must satisfy. Only documents satisfying the WHERE conditions will be returned as part of the query results. It has the following form:

$$\text{WHERE } Term_1 \text{ } \mathcal{LC} \text{ ... } \mathcal{LC} \text{ } Term_n. \tag{2.10}$$

The predicates have the same overall syntax as in WebSQL. Let String denote string, Reg_Exp denote a regular expression, and Tree denote the query tree structure in preorder string format (WAQL represents each document by a tree structure). A term has one of the following four forms:

$$D \text{ mentions String [with dist } OP \text{ } k \text{]}, \tag{2.11}$$

$$D \text{ contains Reg\_Exp}, \tag{2.12}$$

$$D \text{ has Tree [with dist } OP \text{ } k \text{]}, \tag{2.13}$$

and

$$D_1 \text{ -> } D_2 \text{ -> ... -> } D_n. \tag{2.14}$$

Terms of the form (2.11) are used to specify the exact and approximate string matching requirements that resulting documents must satisfy. D is a document pointer that will contain the location of the actual document where string matching will be applied. OP is a comparison operator ($>, <, =$), and k is an integer that specifies the distance allowed for approximate string matching. If k is not specified, a default value of 0 is assumed, which means exact string matching is performed.

Terms of the form (2.12) are used to specify the regular expression matching requirements that resulting documents must satisfy. D is a document pointer containing the location of the actual document where regular expression matching will be applied.

Terms of the form (2.13) are used to specify a hierarchical search query. Once again, D is a document pointer to the location of the actual document where regular expression matching will be applied. OP is a comparison operator, and

k is an integer value that specifies the distance allowed for the approximate tree matching with variable length don't cares (VLDCs). That k equals 0 corresponds to exact-match retrieval, which means the query tree structure must be totally embedded in the document tree structure. That is, a `Tree` T of distance k away from document D is embedded in D if and only if k equals 0. When k is positive, the retrieval is considered to be approximate.

Terms of the form (2.14) are used to specify link constraints. For example, if a term A->B->C is specified then the query requires that document A has a hyperlink to document B and document B has a hyperlink to document C.

In general, terms are not limited to just these four types, but can be any function that resulting documents must satisfy, such as the result of the application of an image or voice recognition algorithm. Thus the query language is flexible and can be extended to incorporate new functions.

3.5 EXAMPLES

Example 1. This query is to find documents containing "database", "oracle", and "relational" using Altavista as the index server. The resulting documents' URLs are returned.

```
select   d.url
using    Altavista d
where    d mentions "database", "oracle", "relational";
```

Example 2. This query is to find documents containing "database" in an H1 tag and a regular expression "object.*relational" in a paragraph using Excite as the index server. This regular expression means the word "object" followed by the word "relational" with a VLDC between these two specified words. Thus, the * matches a string of characters of arbitrary length. The resulting documents' URLs are returned.

```
select   d.url
using    Excite d
where    d has (*(H1("database")(P(*("object.*relational")))));
```

Example 3. This query is to find documents that have the word "database" in an H1 tag, followed by a paragraph containing "oracle", using Infoseek as the index server, and examines only the 23rd to 69th URLs from the list of returned URLs. Most importantly, each matched document must be at most zero or unit

distance away from this hierarchical query pattern in the edit distance sense
defined in [284]. The resulting documents' URLs are returned.

```
select   d.url
using    Infoseek d [23..69]
where    d has (*(H1("database"))(P(*("oracle")))) with dist <= 1;
```

Example 4. This query is to find documents that have the word "RS6000",
and have "deep blue" in the title followed by "kasparov" in a paragraph, where
the search domain is www.ibm.com. The method of search will be depth first
search down to the third level in the Web tree structure.

```
select   d.url
from     http://www.ibm.com d ||> 3
where    d mentions "RS6000" and
         d has (*(title("deep blue"))(P("kasparov")));
```

Example 5. This query is to find books that mention "Ontos", have "database"
in the book title, and put an emphasis on "object database". The author field
in the resulting documents is returned. This query is actually targeting XML
documents because user-defined tags are used.

```
select   d.author
using    index_server d
where    d mentions "Ontos" and
         d has (Book(title("database"))emph("object database"));
```

Chapter 3

MEDIATORS AND WRAPPERS

Search engines and directories, as described in Chapter 1, provide Internet users with rapid retrieval of information, but do not provide a database-like query language to retrieve information based, for example, on the underlying structure of the HTML documents. The lack of such query languages is due largely to the semistructured nature of Web data [1], which is unsuitable for retrieval and storage in a relational database form. Systems based on mediators and data warehouses have been introduced to overcome the inability to query Web data using a full-fledged database query language. In contrast to the approaches described in Chapter 2, which employ search engines as backends, mediators and data warehouses are based on a database management system (DBMS). Thus, the query languages in Chapter 2 would be implemented using search engines and directories as backends. Such a query system would generate, from the user's query, a query or a set of queries that can be executed on the search engines. The responses returned from the search engines would then be compiled and supplied to the user. In the mediator or data warehouse approach, on the other hand, the user interacts with the DBMS, which in turn interacts with the Web.

In the client/server DBMS model, a data server maintains the database. A client sends requests to the server and the server responds by returning a result. Figure 3.1 illustrates a client/server DBMS architecture. Architectures such as mediators and data warehouses have been introduced for a distributed environment where many servers are available. In the data warehouse architecture

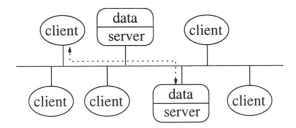

Figure 3.1.   A client/server architecture.

illustrated in Figure 3.2, data are collected from different servers, which may be scattered over a heterogenous wide area network, and integrated into a large data warehouse. The role of the data warehouse is to provide a centralized location to store data and process queries.

Unlike data warehouses, mediators store only a minimal amount of data from various data sources. The goal of a mediator is to provide a centralized location for querying, as opposed to both centralized storage and querying as is done in the case of a data warehouse system.

Both data warehouse and mediator systems use software components, called *wrappers*, to extract data from the Web. The purpose of a wrapper is to filter and transform the Web data into suitable formats. A mediator architecture with wrappers is illustrated in Figure 3.3.

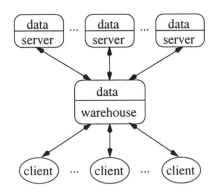

Figure 3.2.   A data warehouse architecture.

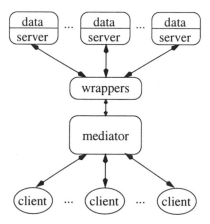

Figure 3.3. A mediator architecture.

Both data warehouse and mediator systems use schemas to model structured data or object models to represent unstructured or semistructured data. The backend of each system is a DBMS which users can query instead of going directly to the Web. The advantage of using a DBMS instead of a Web search engine is that the DBMS has benefits like security and querying facilities. The disadvantage of using a DBMS to store data from the Web is that the domain is limited, because specific programs (wrappers) must be implemented to extract data from different sources. Consequently, users see only that narrow view of the Web which the DBMS is intended to facilitate access to.

In this chapter, we describe systems that use mediators and/or wrappers to integrate databases with the Web. Readers interested in XML should refer to [1, 111]. XML is a new language standard adopted by the World Wide Web Consortium (W3C) [273] that also can handle semistructured data, but unlike mediators and data warehouses, XML does not constitute a system. *WSQ/DSQ* [112] describe another approach that combines the query facilities of a traditional database system with existing search engines on the Web. WSQ, stands for *Web-Supported (Database) Queries*, uses search engine results to enhance SQL queries. DSQ, stands for *Database-Supported (Web) Queries*, uses a database to enhance Web queries. [112] focuses on WSQ.

1.   LORE

Lore (Lightweight Object REpository) [185] is a DBMS designed specifically for managing semistructured information. Unlike traditional database systems that adhere to an explicitly specified schema, Lore can adapt to irregular data with a dynamic schema. Lore includes features such as dynamic structural summaries and seamless access to data from external sources. It uses a query language called Lorel derived by adapting the Object Query Language (OQL) [49] to permit querying semistructured data. Lore uses extensive type coercion and path expressions to query semistructured data effectively.

1.1   OBJECT EXCHANGE MODEL

The data model used by Lore is a self-describing, nested object model called Object Exchange Model (OEM) [2], introduced originally in the TSIMMIS [56] project, a system for integrating heterogeneous data sources. The notion of a fixed schema does not exist in OEM, designed for semistructured data. Data in this model is self-describing in nature and represented by a labeled directed data graph. Schematic information is dynamically embedded on labels assigned to the edges of the data graph.

Figure 3.4 illustrates a simple semistructured database based on the OEM model. The vertices in the graph are objects described by quadruples (`label`, `obj_id`, `type`, `value`) where `label` is a character string; `obj_id` is a unique object identifier; `type` is simple or complex. Simple objects, i.e., atomic objects that have no outgoing edges, contain a `value` from one of the basic atomic types such as `integer`, `float`, `string`, `jpg`, `audio`, etc. Complex objects have outgoing edges with `values` which are either a set or list of `obj_ids`. Special labels, called names, serve as aliases and entry points to the database. Objects not accessible by a path from some name are deleted.

1.2   LOREL

The Lorel query language is the core language of Lore. Lorel is similar to UnQL [44, 45] and uses pattern matching based on the syntax of the semistructured data format. The distinguishing feature of Lorel and UnQL is their ability to search using the data graph. Path expressions are used to specify the search criteria to an arbitrary depth in the data graph. Lorel uses path expressions to return a subset of nodes in the database. Lorel does not construct new nodes, which are the equivalent of a join operation in a relational database, nor test

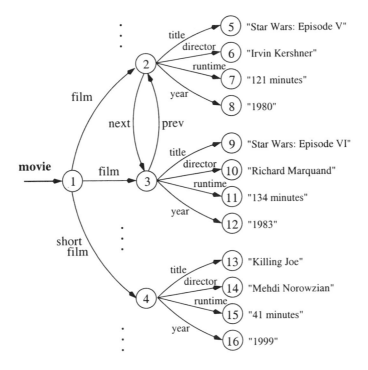

Figure 3.4. An OEM database.

values in the database. The path expression is the basic building block used in finding specific patterns by Lorel.

A path expression is defined as a sequence of edge labels $l_1 . l_2 . ... . l_n$. Its result, as a simple query on a given data graph, is a set of nodes. For example, the result of the path expression "movie.film" in Figure 3.4 is the set of nodes $\{n_i, n_j\}$, where n_i is the movie node and n_j is the film node. The result of the path expression "movie.film.title" is the set of nodes with the associated set of strings like "{..., "Star Wars: Episode VI", "Star Wars: Episode V",...}".

Rather than specify a path explicitly, we can specify it implicitly by imposing desired properties using regular expressions. A property is defined to be either a path property or an edge label. An example of a path/regular expression is "movie.(film|short_film).title", which can match either a film edge or a short_film edge. Let e be a regular expression. An example of a wild card for a regular expression on paths is as follows. Let _ (underscore) denote any edge label, let *e∗* denote a Kleene closure representing an arbitrary number of repetitions of *e*. Then, _* denotes an arbitrary sequence of edges. The expression movie._*.director finds a path that starts with a movie label, ends with a director label, and has any sequence of edges in between. Two more Lorel examples follow:

Example 1. This query searches for film titles with length greater than 2 hours.

```
select   title:   T
from     movie.film F, F.title T, F.runtime N
where    N > 2:00:00;
```

Example 2. This query searches for all information about films or short films directed by "Steven" after the year 1990.

```
select   row:   X
from     movie.(film|short_film) F
where    F.director = "Steven" and F.year > 1990;
```

1.3   ARCHITECTURE

The basic architecture of the Lore system consists of three layers: an Application Program Interface (API) Layer, a Query Compilation Layer, and a Data Engine Layer as shown in Figure 3.5.

The API Layer provides access methods to the Lore system. There is a simple textual interface used primarily by system developers. A graphical interface for end users provides tools for browsing through query results, viewing the structure of data and formulating queries.

The Query Compilation Layer of Lore consists of a Parser, a Preprocessor, a Query Plan Generator, and a Query Optimizer. The Parser takes a query and checks whether it conforms with Lorel's grammar. The Preprocessor is responsible for transforming Lorel queries into OQL-like queries that are easier to process. A query plan is then generated from the transformed query by the Query Plan Generator. The query plan is optimized by the Query Optimizer that decides how to use indexes. The optimized query plan is finally sent to the Data Engine Layer that performs the actual execution of the query.

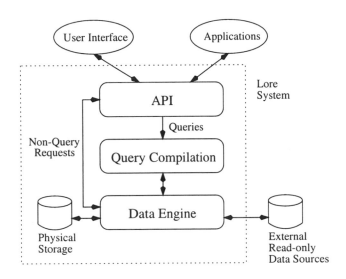

Figure 3.5. Lore architecture.

The **Data Engine Layer** consists of an **Object Manager, Query Operators**, various utilities and an **External Data Manager**. The **Object Manager** is responsible for translation between the OEM data model and the low-level physical storage model. The **Query Operators** are in charge of executing the generated query plans. Utilities include a **Data Guide Manager**, a **Loader** and an **Index Manager**. The **External Data Manager** is responsible for interacting with external read-only data sources.

2. ARANEUS

The ARANEUS [21] project presents a set of languages for managing and restructuring data coming from the WWW. The main objective of ARANEUS is to provide a view to the Web framework. This framework has the following three view levels:

- *Structured view* – Data of interest are extracted from sites and given a database structure.

- *Database view* – Further database views can be generated based on traditional database techniques.

- *Derived hypertext view* – An alternative to the original site can be generated.

In this transformation process, Web data goes from a semistructured organization (Web pages) to a very structured organization (database), then back to a Web format (structured Web pages). Figure 3.6 illustrates the data flow of the transformation process.

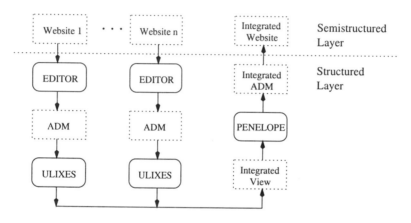

Figure 3.6.   ARANEUS data transformation process.

In order to achieve this transformation, an interesting data model, called the ARANEUS Data Model (ADM), along with two languages ULIXES and PENELOPE are introduced. ADM is used to describe the scheme for a Web hypertext, in the spirit of a database. The ULIXES language is used to define the database view over a site. The PENELOPE language is used to generate a hypertext derived from the database.

2.1   ARANEUS DATA MODEL

ADM is a subset of ODMG [49] based on a page-oriented model which uses a page scheme to extract data from a Website. The notion of a page scheme can be assimilated to the notion of class in ODMG, though list is the only collection type in ADM. ADM also provides a *form* construct for the Web framework, and supports heterogenous union but not inheritance.

The page scheme is used to describe the underlying structure of a set of homogeneous pages in a site. It contains simple and complex attributes. Simple attributes include hyperlinks, images, text and binary data. Complex attributes include lists. The scheme of a Website can be viewed as a collection of connected page schemes. ADM extracts some properties of the pages using this structured Website scheme which provides a high-level description of a Website. The properties are then used as the basis for manipulation.

Text extraction procedures used to extract HTML page information as part of a page scheme, based on the EDITOR language [20], are employed. EDITOR, a language for searching and restructuring text, consists of a set of programs which act as wrappers for extracting and transforming HTML pages from a Website based on page schemes.

An ADM page scheme has the form $P(A_1 : T_1, A_2 : T_2, \ldots, A_n : T_n)$, where P is a page name, each $A_i : T_i$ is an attribute and ADM type pair. An attribute may be labeled *optional* and the page scheme may be labeled as *unique*. Figure 3.7 illustrates a page scheme example [21, 169], declared in the ARANEUS Data Definition Language.

```
PAGE SCHEME AuthorPage
   Name:     TEXT;
   WorkList: LIST OF
        (Authors:    TEXT;
         Title:      TEXT;
         Reference:  TEXT;
         Year:       TEXT;
         ToRefPage:  LINK TO ConferencePage
                        UNION JournalPage;
         AuthorList: LIST OF
                (Name:           TEXT;
                 ToAuthorPage: LINK TO
                        AuthorPage OPTIONAL;););
END PAGE SCHEME
```

Figure 3.7.   AuthorPage scheme for ARANEUS.

In this figure, Name is a uni-valued attribute, and WordList is a multi-valued attribute containing a set of nested tuples that describe the list of publications. For each publication, authors, title, reference, year, link to reference page (conference or journal), and an optional link to each corresponding author page are specified in the scheme. A UNIQUE keyword is assigned to page-schemes that have a single instance in the site as illustrated in Figure 3.8.

```
PAGE SCHEME PageName UNIQUE
...
END PAGE SCHEME
```

Figure 3.8.   A unique page-scheme.

2.2   ULIXES

ULIXES is a language for defining a relational view over the Web. It is designed for extracting data from the Web based on an ADM scheme. The data extraction is based on navigational expressions, also known as path expressions. A DEFINE TABLE statement is used to define a relational view. It has the following form:

```
DEFINE TABLE    γ
AS              η
IN              ξ
USING           α
WHERE           ω
```

where γ specifies a relation $R(a_1, a_2, \ldots, a_n)$, η specifies navigation expressions over ξ; ξ specifies an ADM scheme; α specifies a set of attributes $(A_1, A_2, \ldots, A_n)$ used in ξ that correspond to relation $R(a_1, a_2, \ldots, a_n)$.

As an example, Figure 3.9 illustrates a relational view for VLDB papers used in [21] on the DBLP Bibliography server. In this example, the navigational expression requires that the Submit link returns pages according to scheme AuthorPage. The resulting table contains authors, titles, and references for all papers by Leonardo da Vinci in VLDB conferences.

```
DEFINE TABLE    VLDBPapers (Authors, Title, Reference)
AS              AuthorSearchPage.NameForm.Submit →
                    AuthorPage.WorkList
IN              DBLPScheme
USING           AuthorPage.WorkList.Authors,
                AuthorPage.WorkList.Title
                AuthorPage.WorkList.Reference
WHERE           AuthorSearchPage.NameForm.Name =
                    'Leonardo da Vinci'
                AuthorPage.WorkList.Reference
                    LIKE '%VLDB%';
```

Figure 3.9. Relational view on VLDB papers.

2.3 PENELOPE

PENELOPE is a language for defining new page-schemes according to which data will be organized. It is used to transform relational views back to hypertexts that do not exist in the current site. The derived site can be specified using a DEFINE PAGE statement, which has the following form:

```
DEFINE PAGE    ρ
AS             ξ
FROM           γ
```

where ρ specifies a new page-scheme name and an optional UNIQUE keyword is used to indicate the page-scheme to be unique; ξ specifies the page structure; γ specifies a view that returns a relation $R(a_1, a_2, \ldots, a_n)$.

Taking the example from [21] again, suppose we want to define HTML pages that structure Leonardo da Vinci's papers organized by year as illustrated in Figure 3.10. The structure of the pages can be defined using statements in Figure 3.11. These statements are then used to generate corresponding HTMLs for the new pages. Note that attributes from the source table DaVinciPapers are in < ... >.

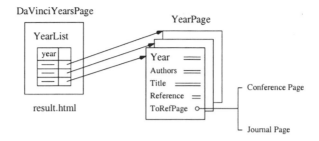

Figure 3.10.   Page-schemes to organize papers by year.

```
DEFINE PAGE DaVinciYearPage UNIQUE
AS  URL       'result.html':
    YearList: LIST OF
         (Year:       TEXT <Year>;
          ToYearPage: LINK TO
                      YearPage (URL(<Year>)));
FROM DaVinciPapers;


DEFINE PAGE YearPage
AS  URL       URL(<Year>);
    Year:     TEXT <Year>;
    WorkList: LIST OF
         (Authors:   TEXT  <Authors>;
          Title:     TEXT  <Title>;
          Reference: TEXT  <Reference>;
          ToRefPage: LINK TO ConferencePage
                     UNION JournalPage;
                       <ToRefPage>);
FROM DaVinciPapers
```

Figure 3.11.   HTML page generating schemes.

3.   AKIRA

The Web is not a database, though retrieved Web pages are cached for faster retrieval. Such Web caching can be viewed as providing a primitive database that captures a view of the Web. A real DBMS can be used to provide database-supported Web caching. Database-supported caching requires Web pages to be stored as a database-supportable unit. Hence, a transformation process on Web pages is required to break Web pages into small pieces. An attempt using object-oriented databases to model HTML pages has been taken by AKIRA [153]. AKIRA introduces the notion of a *fragment*. HTML pages are stored and retrieved as fragments in a database. This database-supported caching can be viewed as a "smart cache" that populates the retrieved content with enriched information. Users can define their own content structure for delivery.

AKIRA integrates information retrieval, browsing, and database techniques into a flexible system for the user. It assumes zero-knowledge on the content source and a predefined schema is not required. The system also defines a query language, PIQL, which is a simple algebra extended with restructuring primitives in a unified framework.

3.1   FRAGMENT DATA MODEL

A fragment is also based on an object model. A fragment corresponds not to a source HTML page, but to a fragment of a page. Thus, an HTML page can be represented by one or more fragments. The structure of the `fragment` class can be represented as shown in Figure 3.12.

```
class Fragment {
   id                          :  Id_type;
   url, content                :  String;
   pred, next, href            :  Fragment;
   href_content, ref_name      :  String;
}
```

Figure 3.12.   A `Fragment` class.

Using this definition of a fragment, an HTML page can be analyzed with finer granularity. In addition, by being able to analyze its contents and implicit structure, the semantics of the original page is preserved. Consider the HTML segment shown in Figure 3.13. It can be partitioned into fragments as listed in Table 3.1.

```
<TITLE>Data Mining</TITLE>
...
<A href="#Web mining">Related Sites</A>
Data Mining Related...
<A name="Web mining">Web Mining</A>
...
```

Figure 3.13.   A segment of HTML.

ID	URL	CONTENT	PRED	NEXT	HREF	HREF_CONTENT	REF_NAME
1	...	"<TITLE>Data..."	null	2	null	""	""
...	...	...	...	...	...		...
5	...	"Related Sites"	4	6	7	"#Web mining"	""
6	...	"Data Mining..."	5	7	null	""	""
7	...	"Related Sites"	6	8	null	""	"Web mining"
...	...	...	...	...	...	...	...

Table 3.1.   A list of HTML fragments generated from the HTML segment in Figure 3.13.

The notion of *concept classes* can be superimposed on that of a `Fragment` class as a component of the database. Concept classes can be used to store domain specific knowledge. A concept class is defined as an abstract class with an attribute REFERS_TO of type `Fragment` that refers to objects of class `Fragment`. Relational concepts can also be defined to express relationships between concepts. Two concept classes, `Person` and MP3 based on the `Fragment` class, are illustrated in Figure 3.14. Concept classes are organized into a hierarchy. New data may be inserted into a new fragment, which is either based on preexisting fragments, or a new instance of concept classes. Using a database to store concept classes provides a database query language with a rich environment for querying a view of the Web. AKIRA also can specify meta-concepts to express relationships between concepts. In Figure 3.14, concept class MP3 is associated with an instance of class `Person`.

```
class Person {                    class MP3 {
   name        :  String;           title       :  String;
   refers_to   :  Fragment;         artist      :  Person;
   ...                              refers_to   :  Fragment;
}                                    ...
                                 }
```

Figure 3.14.   Concept classes for Person and MP3.

3.2   PIQL

PIQL (Path Identity Query Language) is a high-level, OQL-like query language for querying concept classes in AKIRA. It is reminiscent of OQL due to the adoption of an underlying object-oriented database approach. Similarly to Lorel [185], UnQL [44, 45] and POQL [60], it uses path expressions and supports fuzzy search constructs by allowing wild cards and a fuzzy function. The following are PIQL examples.

Example 1. This query is to find Web pages from World Wide Web Consortium that mention XML and return their URLs. The clause y.context = fuzzy("XML") can be used to search for Web pages similar to XML.

```
select   y.url
from     x in Fragment, y in Fragment
where    x.url = "http://www.w3.org/*"
         x.href = y
         y.content = fuzzy("XML");
```

Example 2. This query is to find the artist's name and the title of an MP3 song.

```
select   s.artist.name, s.title
from     s in MP3
         p in Person
where    s.url = p.url
         p in s.artist.refers_to;
```

3.3   ARCHITECTURE

The AKIRA system consists of five components: Dispatcher, Database System, View Factory, Agent Pool, and Output Formatter. Figure 3.15 illustrates the architecture of AKIRA.

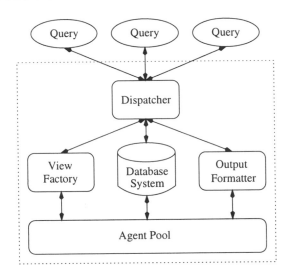

Figure 3.15.   AKIRA system architecture.

The **Dispatcher** has a role similar to the query processor for a DBMS. It is the central component in charge of monitoring processes, taking a query and dispatching it to other components. It also performs query optimizations based on equivalence of algebraic expressions. Its key function in dispatching a query is to match a corresponding schema with elements of the system schema library. The schema is sent to the **Database System** and computable queries to the **View Factory**, which maintains a list of views.

The **Database System** is used to allow efficient retrieval of objects. AKIRA uses an object-oriented database system that utilizes the PIQL language described in this chapter. Its main goal is to store a Web view using concept classes with a class `Fragment` as the base class.

The **Agent Pool** is a repository of services available to other components. AKIRA has an extensible agent architecture where new agents can be dynamically plugged into the system. Agents act as intelligent filters that parse the page content and identify fragments relevant to a query. Agents have the knowledge to identify specific types of information in order to apply the fragmentation process. The **Output Formatter** is the component that is responsible for displaying the result of the query in a user-friendly layout.

Chapter 4

MULTIMEDIA SEARCH ENGINES

Multimedia is integral to both human and modern computer communications. As digital sound and imagery proliferate, the need to search for audio and visual information has increased. However, most popular search engines are still textual as described in Chapter 1, even though the diversity of Web content has transformed the Web from a merely textual to a multimedia-based repository. Web information content comes in a variety of audio, video, image, and text formats, a list of the most commonly found media formats and types being given in Table 4.1. The multimedia information is highly distributed, minimally indexed, and lacks appropriate schemas. The critical question in multimedia search is how to design a scalable, visual information retrieval system? Such audio and visual information systems require large resources for transmission, storage and processing, factors which make indexing, retrieving, and managing visual information an immense challenge.

Progress has recently been made in developing and deploying efficient, effective, easy to use, mass-scale multimedia content search engines. Commercial search systems include AltaVista Photo Finder [13], Lycos Pictures and Sounds [174], scour.net [233], Yahoo! Image Surfer [276], Ditto [80], Stream Search [253], Midi Explorer [192], Lycos Fast MP3 Search [173], MP3 [198], and Sound Crawler [245]. Research prototypes for multimedia search engines include AMORE [15, 199, 200], WebSeek [55, 242, 265] and WebSeer [255, 266].

Media Format	File Extension	Media Type
Midi	`midi`	Audio
MP3	`mp3`	Audio
RealAudio	`ra,ram`	Audio
WAV Audio	`wav`	Audio
AVI	`avi`	Video
MPEG Video	`mpeg,mpg,mpe,mpv,mpegv`	Video
QuickTime	`qt,mov,moov`	Video
RealMedia	`ra,ram`	Video
MPEG Audio	`mp2,mpa,abs,mpega`	Video
PNG Image	`png`	Image
Windows Bitmap	`bmp`	Image
X Bitmap	`xbm`	Image
TIFF Image	`tiff,tif`	Image
JPEG Image	`jpeg,jpg,jpe`	Image
GIF Image	`gif`	Image
PDF	`pdf`	Document
TeX DVI Data	`dvi`	Document
Postscript	`ai,eps,ps`	Document

Table 4.1.   Media types and file extensions.

There are three categories of techniques for multimedia searching on the Web: text or keyword-based techniques, semantics or content-based techniques, or techniques based on a combination of both.

- *Text or Keyword-based* – User can specify keywords, and multimedia relevant to the specified keywords can be retrieved. For example, find all images on `cars`.

- *Semantics or Content-based* – User can specify search criteria based on the semantic content of the multimedia object (image, audio, or video). For example, retrieve images visually similar to a given image. This is done using various image processing techniques.

- *Keyword and Content-based* – User can specify both keywords and content-based search criteria, combining the first two techniques.

This chapter surveys some of the most widely used techniques in multimedia searching on the Web. Though text is an inseparable part of a multimedia system, we refer the reader to Chapter 1 for a discussion of its retrieval and index methods.

1.   TEXT OR KEYWORD-BASED SEARCH

Text or keyword-based multimedia search systems require an inverted file index to describe the multimedia content. The index is needed for fast query response, just as for keyword-based information search discussed in Chapter 1. Thus, building an index is at the heart of keyword-based multimedia searching.

Another important indexing technique used in multimedia search engines is partitioning multimedia content into categories, which the user can browse through for images of interest that match category keywords. Keywords can also be specified for finding similar images.

Identifying the text that describes content is essential to the cataloging and indexing process. The relationship between images and their textual captions in large photographic libraries like newspaper archives has been examined in [225, 249]. The lack of captions for multimedia content on the Web has led to efforts to develop indexes and searchable catalogs based on associated textual content such as the Web address and hyperlink reference text.

The use of the text embedded around multimedia content as a way of identifying its content is an approach born of necessity because automatically categorizing a media item based on its content is not an easy process. For example, in the case of an image, it requires image analysis using pattern recognition, feature extraction, and shape analysis algorithms, which are still wide open areas of research. Therefore, rather than applying complex visual analysis algorithms, models based on the text content and hyperlink structure surrounding the multimedia content have been proposed.

A variety of techniques have been developed for assigning keywords to multimedia content on the Web. For example, the URL and HTML tags associated with the images are considered in [55, 242]; text in the center tag within the same table cell is used in [255]; text after an image URL is used in [122]; and text "near" an image is used in [200, 226]. This section discusses all these techniques.

1.1   KEYWORDS ASSIGNMENT

Multimedia content, especially images, can be incorporated into HTML documents. The ability to link either text or images to another document or section of a document makes HTML very powerful. Very importantly, every image on the Web has a unique Web address (URL) and possibly some associated text that describes the image. The text close to an image therefore may be useful for characterizing and describing the content of the image. Images can thus be indexed or cataloged by using the following kinds of methods based on the surrounding text and hyperlink structure:

- Key Term Extraction.

- Directory Name Extraction.

There is a variety of information available on an HTML page to be used as a basis for assigning keywords to images. Key term extraction and directory name extraction can then be applied to categorize the image using text information in the tags and hypertext. The same techniques can be applied to audio and video files.

In key term extraction, terms are extracted from the hyperlink_text and the ALT tag field by chopping the text at non-alphabet characters. For example, consider the expression:

```
"vehicle/cars/nice_car.html" = "vehicle", "cars", and "nice car".
```

A search engine can index the terms extracted for the images using an inverted file as shown in Figure 4.1.

In directory name extraction, the name of a directory is extracted from the URL in tag fields such as HREF and SRC. The directory names are used to map images to subject classes based on a key-term dictionary.

A *key-term dictionary* is a set of key-terms and their corresponding mapping to subject classes. The key-terms are identified either manually or semi-manually by criteria such as frequency count. The mapping from key-terms to subjects also can be automatically or semi-automatically established.

Some common sources for key term and directory name extractions are as follows:

- Anchor tag – used to create links to other documents or images.

- Image tag – used to create inline images in a document.

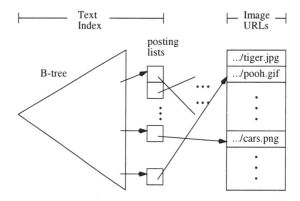

Figure 4.1.   Keyword-image inversion index.

- Heading tag – used to specify six levels of headers for a document.

- Title tag – used to specify a document title.

- Table tag – used to format a table.

- Document text – used to describe the content of images.

Anchor Tag

Images on the Web are published in two forms: referenced and inlined. A referenced image from a parent document uses the <A> tag, which stands for anchor. An anchor is an area in a document where a mouse click will link to the specified URL. The <A> tag has the following general format:

```
<A   HREF    = "URL"
     NAME    = "text"
     REL     = ["next"|"previous" ... ]
     REV     = [ "next"|"previous" ... ]
     TITLE   = "text" >    hyperlink_text    </A>
```

The HREF is used to specify the URL to be linked to when this hyperlink is clicked. This URL can be any legal URL, including images, sounds, etc. By specifying a NAME field, a specific location in the document will be accessible via another URL. The relationship between the URL specified in HREF and this document can be specified in the REL and REV attributes. REL defines the forward relationship between this document and the HREF URL; and REV defines the reverse relationship between the HREF URL and this document. The TITLE of the anchor can also be specified. The clickable area would be the hyperlink_text which describes the object pointed to by the hyperlink.

Image Tag

The ability to display inlined images is one of the most powerful features of HTML. Image types supported by Web browsers include BMP, GIF, JPEG and PNG. The HTML for including an image has the following general form:

```
<IMG   SRC      = "URL"
       ALT      = "text"
       WIDTH    = "pixels"
       HEIGHT   = "pixels"
       ALIGN    = ["top"|"middle" ... ]
       ISMAP    = "pixels"                        >
```

The SRC specifies the URL, which is the location of the image. For text-only browsers such as Lynx, which cannot display graphic images, or for users who might have turned off image loading due to slow Internet connections, HTML provides a mechanism for displaying text in place of the missing images by using the ALT tag. Image size is specified in pixels using WIDTH and HEIGHT tags. Alignment can be specified in an ALIGN tag to align subsequent text. If ISMAP is specified, and an anchor surrounds the image, then the image is treated as a clickable map. That is, the coordinates of the mouse click will be processed by browser script or returned to the parsing script specified by the anchor's URL.

Inlined images can also be used as hyperlinks just like plain text. After an image becomes inlined it is clickable just like regular hypertext. The following HTML code illustrates how to make an image called bird.gif inlined:

```
<A HREF="URL"><IMG SRC="bird.gif" ALT="Bird Image"></A>
```

The URL field in both <A> and <IMG> tags has the following form, where [. . .] denotes an optional argument:

```
http://host.site.domain[:port]/[dirs/][file[.extension]]
```

Heading Tag
HTML headings in H{1-6} tags may also contain useful text information about images. Depending on the location of the images, some headings will tend to be less relevant to the image content. If an image is in heading Hi, the text for a previous heading Hj, where $j \leq i$, can be ignored [199]. For example, image "image.gif" in the <IMG> tag in the following HTML source is more relevant to heading <H3>Section 1.1.1</H3> than to the other headings.

```
<HTML>
...
<H1>Chapter 1</H1>
    <H2>Section 1.1</H2>
        ...
        <H3>Section 1.1.1</H3>
            ...
            <IMG SRC="image.gif">
        ...
    <H2>Section 1.2</H2>
        ...
</HTML>
```

Title Tag
HTML <TITLE> tags can also be used to help identify the semantics of images on a page [255], since the title tag is used to display a page title in the browser title bar. But, <TITLE> tags may not be useful when the images on a page have diverse content because they might not be directly related to the title.

Table Tag
Images can be formatted using the HTML <TABLE> tag. If the caption of an image is in the same cell as the image, then the caption can be used as an accurate description of the image [255]. But this method is likely to

fail when the relevant text for the image is found in another cell. A more sophisticated approach can be applied to determine the corresponding image caption within the table cells. Captions within a table usually follow the same scheme. Caption alignment schemes within a table can then be determined by parsing the entire table and finding a regular pattern within it [199].

Document Text

Document text surrounding an image in a Web page may also be relevant to identifying image content. Determining which part of the text surrounding an image is relevant is a challenging problem because associated text can be aligned in many different ways. Image captions can occur before, after, or both before and after an image. A variety of approaches have been proposed for solving this image caption alignment problem.

For example, the text after an image URL until the end of a paragraph (<P> tag) or the text up to where there is a link to another image (<IMG> tag) can be taken as the caption of the image [122]. Line breaks (
 tag) have also been used [199] to define the visual closeness of a text to an image. Another approach is to use the text near an image, where *nearness* is defined as text lying within a fixed number of lines or words in an HTML document source file [226].

In situations where a text is simultaneously near two images, syntactical comparison can be applied [199]. The syntactical comparison can, for example, find the closeness between an image file name in the URL and the surrounding text. *Closeness*, defined as the syntactic distance d between the image file name f and the text t, is given by:

$$d(f, t) = \frac{c(f, t)}{|f|}$$

where $|f|$ is the number of characters in the string f, and $c(f, t)$ is the number of characters in f that also occur as a string in t in the same order.

1.2   SUBJECT TAXONOMY

The information extracted using the methods described in Section 1.1 in this chapter can be used to classify images into different subject classes. A subject class is an ontological concept that describes the semantic content of an image or video. Using an is-a hierarchy, the subject class can be arranged

- Arts   - Recreation
- Entertainment   - Science
- People   - Vehicles

Table 4.2.   Categories of Yahoo! Image Surfer.

into a subject taxonomy. When a new and descriptive term is detected, it will be added to the taxonomy if it does not already exist. Table 4.2 shows top level subject classes (categories) available at Yahoo! Image Surfer [276], which is powered by Excalibur's Image Surfer [88]. For example, the Art category contains subcategories like architecture, ceramics, dance, painting, while the Science category contains subcategories like animals, space and astronomy.

A catalog database can be built using subject classes and keywords with the following tables:

```
TYPE (ID, TYPE)
IMAGES (ID, URL, FORMAT, WIDTH, HEIGHT)
SUBJECT (ID, SUBJECT)
CONTENT (ID, TERM)
```

The following SQL query can be used to retrieve images of painting by Van Gogh.

```
select   ID
from     TYPE, SUBJECT, CONTENT
where    TYPE = "image" AND
         SUBJECT = "painting" AND
         TERM = "Van Gogh";
```

2.   CONTENT-BASED SEARCH

The text provided in the directory name and the hyperlink text described in the preceding section can produce an effective image search engine. However, by examining the image content, we can substantially refine the search results as well as provide more search features. Many systems use such techniques to overcome the shortcomings of keyword-based image search tools.

One of the first systems that allowed users to find images similar to a given image was the Query By Image Content (QBIC) [102]. It has attracted considerable attention because it allows finding images based on a given image's color and texture. The notion of image similarity was extended by Markus Stricker at ETH to include fuzzy color matching and fuzzy regions in an image. Image databases discussed in [214, 227] introduced image indexing techniques to find similar images. The Virage [22] system for image retrieval is based on visual features consisting of low level primitives, such as color, shape, texture and possibly domain specific features.

WebSeek [242] performs content-based search for images using color histograms generated from visual scenes. The color histograms describe the distribution of colors in an image. Image similarity is determined based on the color histogram of each image. The weighted dissimilarity between histograms is calculated using dissimilarity functions. An image type assessment is automatically done using Fisher discriminant analysis to construct a series of uncorrelated linear weightings of the color histograms. This analysis provides maximum separation between training classes. Feedback from the user can also be used to reformulate a query to obtain better results, based on the principle that users are after all the best judges for determining the relevance of retrieved images.

A system called AMORE [15] uses a Content-Oriented Image Retrieval (COIR) library and allows a content-based query to specify images containing certain object shapes. AMORE has two subsystems: an indexing engine and a matching engine. The indexing engine is used to index identified shapes in images and the matching engine is used to search for images that match the shapes given in a query, as discussed in Section 2.1 in this chapter.

The indexing and retrieval complexity associated with audio and video content search has thus far impeded the large scale use of multimedia search engines on the Web. Therefore, most audio and video search engines are still text-based. In this section, we will discuss three popular techniques used in image similarity based search: shape analysis, color analysis, and texture analysis.

2.1   SHAPE ANALYSIS

Shape analysis is the process of extracting objects from images. The process subdivides the original image into regions based on color, edge, position, and texture using image processing techniques like edge detection, color analysis and region division. Each region has a set of attributes such as color, shape, texture, size, object location and object composition. The extracted attribute values are stored as metadata to be used during the matching process. Figure 4.2 shows the objects extracted from an image.

Figure 4.2. Object extraction from an image.

Objects extracted from images come in a wide variety of shapes and sizes, so it is a nontrivial issue as to how to cluster extracted objects. Predefined shapes such as circles, ellipses, triangles, rectangles, and squares of different sizes and aspect ratios may be used as templates for clustering seeds, as illustrated in Figure 4.3. An object only needs to be similar to a seed shape in order to be added to the corresponding cluster.

When a query image is specified for which one seeks to find similar images, the attribute values associated with the query image are extracted and stored as metadata. This metadata is then compared with image metadata in the database of indexed images and results are returned based on the matching scores of the comparison. Queries can also be formulated to find images containing certain shapes.

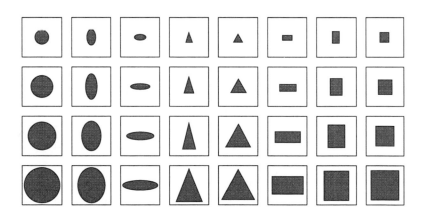

Figure 4.3. Shape templates for clustering seeds.

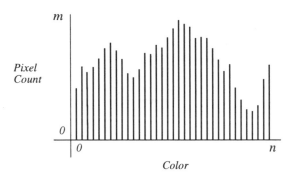

Figure 4.4.   Color histogram.

2.2   COLOR ANALYSIS

Another technique for representing the image content or characterizing an image is the *color histogram* [254]. A color histogram describes the color distribution in an image or video scene. A quantized HSV color space is typically used to represent the color. A color histogram $H(M)$ is denoted as a vector $(h_1, h_2, \ldots, h_n)$ in an n-dimensional vector space, where each h_c represents the number of pixels of color c in the image M. Figure 4.4 illustrates a color histogram. Given two color histograms, α and β, a function that measures the weighted dissimilarity between them can be defined as:

$$sim(\alpha, \beta) = 1 - \sum_{i=1}^{n} min(\alpha[i], \beta[i]),$$

where n is the number of bins used in the histogram, and $\alpha[i]$ and $\beta[i]$ are h_i in α and β vectors respectively. This method can be used to accurately and efficiently measure the (dis)similarity between two images based on color [243]. However, this method is not able to capture semantic information because two images can have similar color histograms but with different contents.

2.3   TEXTURE ANALYSIS

Texture analysis is another method of determining the similarity between images. The most commonly used features to represent texture are *coarseness, contrast, and directionality* (CCD) as developed in [92, 256].

- Coarseness – a measure of granularity of the texture.

- Contrast – a measure of the distribution of luminance.

- Directionality – a measure of the direction of an image.

An enhanced version of CCD using histogram-based features to reduce noise is described in [186]; and various content-based query models over image databases are discussed in [209].

II
DATA MINING ON THE WEB

Chapter 5

DATA MINING

Advances in storage, networking, processing power, and software technology have enabled us to efficiently store and retrieve digital data in databases, data warehouses, or other information repositories. *What can we do with this accumulated data?* Ignoring this data would be wasteful because much of the needed knowledge is waiting to be discovered in the repositories. The underlying thesis of data mining is to use techniques to discover and extract valuable knowledge in this data. The vast amount of data on the Web, in particular, has made data exploration tools essential. This chapter presents the basic concepts of data mining and knowledge discovery in databases.

1. WHAT IS DATA MINING?

Informally speaking, data mining is the process of extracting information or knowledge from a data set for the purposes of decision making [94]. Data mining has become a very active field in recent years because of the wide availability of large data sets. The information and knowledge gained from data mining can be used in areas ranging from scientific research to market analysis. Data mining is an evolutionary step in the development of database and information technology, fields which have evolved from primitive file processing systems in the 1960s to database management systems, to advanced data warehousing and data mining systems.

In the 1960s, file systems used flat files to store and retrieve data. The inefficiencies of flat files led to the development of database systems in the 1970s, including network and relational databases, using a variety of data modeling, indexing and data organization techniques, and supported by high-level query languages. Since the mid-1980s, vast effort has been expended on research into and development of enhanced database systems. Based on more advanced data modeling techniques, such as extended-relational, object-relational, object-oriented, deductive and semistructured models, application-oriented database systems, including active, multimedia, spatial, temporal, document, scientific, knowledge-based and information retrieval systems have flourished. In the 1990s, heterogeneous, distributed database systems, followed by global information systems, such as the Web, have played a key role in the information industry.

The volume of data and our inability to comprehend large sets of data have prompted the development of more powerful analytical tools for on-line analytical processing (OLAP) and data mining (DM), which will be discussed in Sections 2 and 3 in this chapter.

As said earlier, data mining refers to the extraction or discovery of knowledge from large amounts of data. Other terms with similar meaning include knowledge mining, knowledge extraction, data analysis and pattern analysis. The main difference that separates information access apart from data mining is their goals. Information access is to help users search for documents or data that satisfy their information needs [23]. Data mining is beyond just search; it discovers useful knowledge by analyzing data correlations using sophisticated data mining techniques.

The kind of knowledge that can be mined using OLAP and DM techniques includes: concept description, association rules, classification and prediction, and clustering. In the context of text and Web mining, the knowledge includes word association, trend, event, browsing behavior, and online communities, which will be discussed in Chapters 6 and 7.

2.   ON-LINE ANALYTICAL PROCESSING

Advances in computer hardware technology over the past three decades have made possible a new architecture called the data warehouse that was briefly introduced in Chapter 3. A data warehouse is an integrated, subject-oriented, collection of nonvolatile historical data [138]. With this architecture, data now can come from many different types of databases with multiple heterogeneous data sources.

Data warehousing has led to the development of on-line analytical processing (OLAP), which is used to analyze vast amount of data to assist in decision making. OLAP uses statistical techniques and multidimensional data cubes to view information from different angles as illustrated in Figure 5.1. OLAP data cube operations in Figure 5.1 include:

- *Dice* – performs selection on one or more dimensions of a given data cube (dice for *School* = "B" or "C" and *Year* = 1997 or 1996 and *Major* = "English" or "Math").

- *Slice* – performs selection on one dimension of a given data cube (slice for *Year* = 1986).

- *Rotate* – performs rotation/pivoting on data axes of a given data cube.

- *Roll-up* – performs dimension reduction or concept hierarchy ascension on a given data cube (roll-up on *Year* from single year to decade).

- *Drill-down* – performs dimension expansion based on concept hierarchy on a given data cube (drill-down on *Major* to more detailed categories).

Although OLAP tools support multidimensional data analysis and decision making, additional analysis tools are needed to conduct in-depth analysis, such as classification, information extraction, especially for data that changes over time. Tremendous amounts of data are stored on the Web. This rapidly growing Web repository combined with the data stored in databases has far exceeded our ability to comprehend it. Data mining is now an indispensable tool in performing data analysis to uncover important data patterns, hence, greatly improving business strategy decision [30] and scientific research results [261].

3. PATTERN EXTRACTION PROCESSES

Some researchers view data mining as synonymous with knowledge discovery in databases (KDD), while others consider it only as an important step in the process of KDD. The knowledge discovery process consists of the following steps:

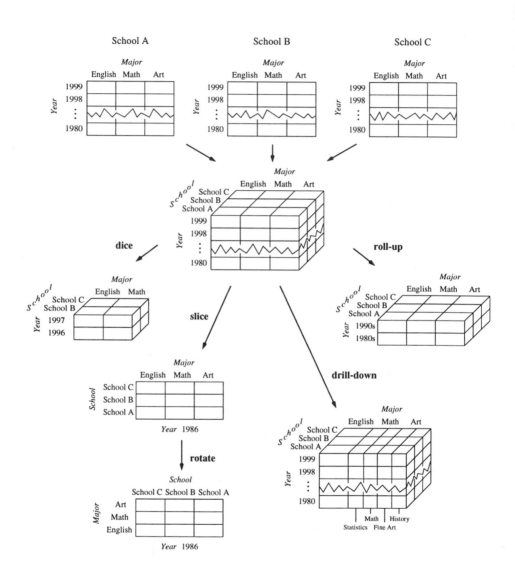

Figure 5.1.   A 3-D data cube and OLAP operations.

- *Data cleaning* - cleans *dirty* data including *incomplete* data (where there are missing attribute values or attributes), *noise* (incorrect or unexpected values), and *inconsistent* data (containing value and attribute name discrepancies). Dirty data obviously contributes to inaccurate analysis and incorrect results.

- *Data integration* - combines data from multiple sources including multiple databases, which might have different content and formats. Inconsistent formats can lead to redundancy and inconsistency in attribute and data values.

- *Data transformation* - transforms data into appropriate and consistent formats using methods such as aggregation (summation), normalization, and smoothing.

- *Data reduction* - reduces data size while retaining the integrity of the original data set. Strategies include data cube aggregation (e.g. sum() and min()), dimension reduction (irrelevant and weak attribute removal), data compression (replacing data values with alternative data encoding), numerosity reduction (replacing data values with smaller alternative representation), and data generalization (replacing data values of low conceptual levels with higher conceptual levels).

- *Data mining* - intelligently extracts data patterns.

- *Pattern evaluation* - identifies truly interesting patterns that represent knowledge using techniques including statistical analysis and query languages.

- *Knowledge presentation* - presents extracted knowledge using visualization and knowledge representation techniques, including graphs, charts, tables, and rules.

The first four steps are known as data *preprocessing* or *preparation* [147, 218, 267]. This book discusses only pattern extraction techniques for data mining in the KDD process. For details of the other steps and related background introduction, refer to [29, 95, 120, 191, 195, 213, 267, 269]. In the following subsections, we describe some major pattern extraction processes for data mining.

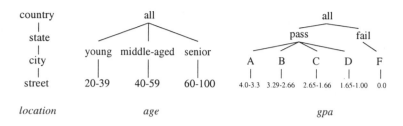

Figure 5.2.   Concept hierarchy.

3.1   CONCEPT DESCRIPTION

Large amounts of data are stored in databases in rigorous structure. Query facilities provide a way of filtering and retrieving data. However, for some users, a concise summary of information extracted from the data which cannot be achieved by simple enumeration or manipulation of the data, is more desired. For example, a manager may like to have an overall picture of a class of market data or a comparison among sets of classes of data. This kind of descriptive data mining is called *concept description* [62, 77, 190].

Concept description can be divided into *characterization analysis* or *discrimination analysis*. Characterization analysis provides concise summaries of sets of data. Discrimination analysis provides descriptive comparisons between sets of data.

Data in databases often stores detailed low-level concept information. The characterization process provides data generalization and summarization to transform task-relevant data from a lower conceptual level to higher conceptual levels. In addition to making discovered patterns easier to understand, it also compresses the data by using fewer terms. Figure 5.2 illustrates a concept hierarchy for the attributes "location", "age", and "gpa" where the concepts range from high-level concepts towards the root of the hierarchy tree to low-level concepts at the leaves of the hierarchy tree.

Data generalization of large data sets uses either a data cube [64] or an attribute-oriented induction (AOI) approach [47, 121]. The data cube approach uses rolling up by replacing low-level concepts with higher-level concepts as described in Section 2 of this chapter. In the AOI approach, generalization is performed either by *attribute removal* or *attribute generalization* based on the concept hierarchy. An attribute may be removed either because there are too

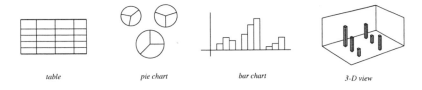

table   *pie chart*   *bar chart*   *3-D view*

Figure 5.3.   Visualization methods for generalized data.

many distinct values for the attribute and no concept hierarchy is defined for it, or because it can be expressed in terms of other attributes in its higher-level hierarchy. For example, removal of the "street" attribute in a location concept is a form of generalization because the "city" and "state" attributes may be adequately to express the concept. Attribute generalization can use the concept hierarchy to replace an attribute with higher-level concepts, a procedure called concept tree ascension.

Data generalization is data dependent because some attributes may remain at a low abstraction level while others are removed or replaced with higher levels. Two techniques, which are based on threshold control, can be applied either individually or in combination to determine whether to remove or generalize an attribute. The first technique is called *attribute generalization threshold control*, in which the threshold is compared with the number of distinct values for an attribute. The second technique is called *relation generalization threshold control*, in which the threshold is compared with the number of distinct tuples in a relation.

Generalized data can be visualized using tables, pie chart, bar chart, or 3-D view as illustrated in Figure 5.3, or can be represented using logic-based characterization rules.

Attribute relevance analysis can be utilized to automated generalization process and mining class discriminations. An attribute within a class is considered highly relevant if its values can be easily used to distinguish one class from another. For example, it is more feasible to distinguish graduate students from undergraduate students using the "age" attribute (high relevance) than by using the "major" attribute (low relevance). There are many models for assessing attribute relevance.

Discrimination analysis attempts to mine distinguishing characteristics that differentiate a target class from comparable contrasting classes. In this terminology, "person" and "CD title" are not comparable classes, while "graduate students" and "undergraduate students" are comparable. Discrimination analysis uses data attribute relevance, generalization, and presentation of derived comparisons in appropriate visualization diagrams or via discriminant rules. The comparison typically involves aggregate functions (count(), sum(), avg(), min(), and max()) and statistical models.

3.2   ASSOCIATION RULE MINING

Association rule mining [5, 7, 180] is the process of finding interesting correlation among a large set of data items. For example, the discovery of interesting association relationships in large volumes of business transactions can facilitate decision making in marketing and Website structure design.

A typical example of association rule mining is *purchasing analysis*, which analyzes customer buying habits by discovering associations among items purchased by customers. For instance, identifying frequently purchased item pairs can help retailers develop marketing strategies to promote merchandising.

An association rule discovered in computer bookstore transactions may look as follows:

$$\text{Operating System} \Rightarrow \text{Linux} \quad [\textit{support} = 3\%, \textit{confidence} = 45\%]$$

This rule reflects a purchasing pattern for computer books: customers who purchase Operating System books tend to buy Linux books at the same time. *Support* and *confidence* are two measures that reflect the usefulness and certainty of the discovered rule. A support of 3% means that 3% of all the transactions in the analysis show that Operating System books and Linux books are purchased together. A confidence of 45% means that 45% of the customers who purchased an Operating System book also bought a Linux book.

Formally, association is defined as follows: Let $I = \{i_1, i_2, \ldots, i_m\}$ be a set of items and $T = \{t_1, t_2, \ldots, t_n\}$ be a set of transactions such that each t_i is a subset of I. Let X be a set of items. A transaction t_i is said to contain X if and only if X is a subset of t_i. An association rule is an implication of the form $X \Rightarrow Y$, where $X \subseteq I$, $Y \subseteq I$, and $X \cap Y = \phi$. The rule $X \Rightarrow Y$ holds in the transaction set T with a support δ and confidence α. The support δ is defined as the percentage of transactions in T that contain $X \cup Y$. The δ is an approximation for the probability $P(X \cup Y)$. The confidence α is defined as the percentage of transactions in T containing X that also contain Y. The α approximates the conditional probability $P(Y|X)$.

Association rules are typically considered interesting if they satisfy two user defined constraints: a minimum support threshold (min-δ) and a minimum confidence threshold (min-α). Association rules not satisfying these constraints are considered statistically insignificant.

Let us refer to a set of items as an itemset. Association rule mining can be described as a two-step process:

1. Find all frequent itemsets that satisfy (min-δ), a pre-determined minimum support.

2. Generate association rules that satisfy (min-α), a pre-determined minimum confidence, from the frequent itemsets discovered in Step 1.

This type of association mining is called *single-dimensional association mining*. Variants include *multidimensional association mining* [143], which mines associations containing multiple predicates of the form $X, Y \Rightarrow Z$; *multilevel association mining* [118, 250], which mines associations among data items at different abstraction levels and discovers patterns among different abstraction spaces; *quantitative (or distance-based) association mining* [166, 193, 251, 281], which mines associations using approximate data values; and *constraint-based association mining* [115, 156, 206], which mines associations based on some predefined constraints.

3.3 CLASSIFICATION AND PREDICTION

Data classification and data prediction are two types of data analysis that can be used to classify data and predict trends. Roughly speaking, data *classification* predicts class labels while data *prediction* predicts continuous-valued functions. Typical applications include risk analysis for loans and growth prediction.

Data classification involves two-steps: *learning* and *classification*. In the learning step, a model is used to analyze a training data set composed of training data tuples or samples that are randomly selected from a sample population. This is also called *supervised learning* because a class label is pre-assigned to each training tuple prior to initiation of the learning process.

In the second step, the model is used for classification. The predictive accuracy of the model is first estimated using class-labelled, randomly selected test samples (test set). The predicted class label for each test sample is compared with its predetermined label. The accuracy of the model is defined as

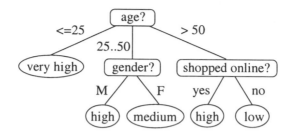

Figure 5.4.   A decision tree for the concept "online shopping".

the percentage of test samples which are correctly classified. If the accuracy is acceptable, the model can then be used to classify unknown objects to their appropriate classes. Otherwise, the model is modified until it satisfies an acceptable level of classification accuracy.

Major techniques for data classification include:

Decision Trees

A decision tree [201, 219] is a flow-chart-like tree structure, whose internal nodes represent test attributes and whose leaf nodes correspond to classes or concepts that represent a prediction. Each branch in the tree corresponds to a decision resulting from a test performed in the adjacent internal node. Unknown samples are classified via the decision tree test. A test walk is defined as a path from the root to a leaf node. Decision trees can be easily converted to classification rules using an if-then-else construct. Figure 5.4 illustrates a decision tree which predicts the likelihood an Internet user will shop online. Internal test nodes are denoted by rounded rectangles and leaf nodes, which indicate the propensity to shop online, are denoted by ovals and correspond to the identified class.

Bayesian Classification

Bayesian classifiers [82]   are statistical classifiers based on Bayes theorem in probability theory.   Let X be a data sample whose class label is unknown.   Let H be some hypothesis such that data sample X belongs to class C.   The probability that H holds on data sample X is the posterior probability defined as $P(H|X)$. In contrast, $P(H)$ is the prior probability of H, which is independent of X.   Similarly, $P(X|H)$ is the posterior probability of X

conditioned on H. $P(X)$ is the prior probability of X. Bayes theorem is defined as:

$$P(H|X) = \frac{P(X|H)P(H)}{P(X)}.$$

Based on Bayes theorem, *naive Bayesian classifiers* [268] and *Bayesian belief networks* [127] are developed. Naive Bayesian classifiers assume class conditional independence, that is, an attribute value for a given class is independent of the values of the other attributes. Bayesian belief networks in contrast allow dependencies among subsets of attributes, which they represent graphically.

k-Nearest Neighbor

Nearest neighbor classifiers store all training samples, not building a classifier until a new sample needs to be classified. Each training sample is interpreted as a point in an n-dimensional pattern space. When an unknown sample is given, a k-nearest neighbor classifier searches the n-dimensional pattern space for the k nearest points based on the Euclidean distance between two points. Given two points $X = (x_1, x_2, \ldots, x_n)$, $Y = (y_1, y_2, \ldots, y_n)$, and a perceived important weight for each variable $W = (w_1, w_2, \ldots, w_n)$, the *Euclidean distance* and the *weighted* Euclidean distance are defined as:

$$d(X,Y) = \sqrt{\sum_{i=1}^{n}(x_i - y_i)^2} \quad and \quad d(X,Y) = \sqrt{\sum_{i=1}^{n} w_i(x_i - y_i)^2}.$$

Another well-known metric is the *Manhattan (or city block) distance*, defined as:

$$d(X,Y) = \sum_{i=1}^{n}(|x_i - y_i|).$$

The unknown sample is assigned to the most common class among its k nearest neighbors. Lazy learners, such as the k-nearest neighbor classifier, can incur expensive computational costs during the neighbor finding process, so they require efficient indexing techniques.

Other common classification techniques include: neural networks [128] which use backpropagation as a learning network model, association rule mining [6] as discussed in Section 3.2 of this chapter, genetic algorithms [110, 194] which use ideas of natural selection as the learning model to train sample data, rough sets [61, 211, 286] which are used to approximate model classes or concepts using equivalence classes, fuzzy sets [31, 282] which use fuzzy logic to allow fuzzy thresholds or vague boundaries rather than having precise cut-offs.

Prediction of continuous values instead of categorical labels can be modeled using the statistical techniques of regression [9, 140, 141, 212]. Regression models include *linear regression,* which estimates behavior using a linear model; *multiple regression* for multidimensional feature vectors; *polynomial regression* for nonlinear models; *logistic regression* which is used to model the probability of events occurring as a linear function of a set of predictor variables; *Poisson regression* for data assumed to follow a Poisson distribution; and the *log-linear model* which approximates discrete multidimensional probability distributions.

3.4   CLUSTERING

A cluster is a collection of mutually similar data objects. Clustering is the process of grouping data objects into clusters [123, 139, 146]. Clustering analysis has a wide range of applications, including image processing, business transaction analysis, and pattern recognition.

In contrast to classification, where a class label is known for each object, object class labels are not pre-given in clustering. Hence, clustering is also known as *unsupervised learning.* The objective of clustering is to enable one to discover distribution patterns and correlations among data objects by identifying dense versus sparse regions in the data distribution.

Major techniques for clustering include:

Partitioning
Partitioning separates n objects into k groups called partitions, where each partition represents a cluster. Partitioning assumes that (1) $k \leq n$, (2) each partition must contain at least one object, and (3) each object must be a member of some partition (more than one partition is allowed if fuzzy partitioning techniques [32, 146] are used). Partitioning methods typically create an initial partition, which is then refined using iterative relocation techniques (IRT) to improve the partitioning. IRT improves

the partitioning by moving objects from one group to another. Heuristics are used to avoid exhaustive enumeration of all possible partitions, such as the *k-means* method [175], where each cluster is represented by the mean value of the objects in the cluster, and the *k-medoids* method [146], where each cluster is represented by a close-to-center object, which is used to represent the cluster in comparisons. Variants include the *k-modes* method which is used to cluster categorical data, and the *k*-prototypes method used to cluster hybrid data [134]. The expectation maximization (EM) method [159] uses weight based measures to assign each data object with different probabilities to every cluster instead of just one cluster.

Hierarchical
Hierarchical methods [117, 145, 146] construct a hierarchical decomposition of the given set of data objects using either an agglomerative or a divisive method.   In the *agglomerative* approach, the algorithm starts with each object as its own cluster. It successively merges similar clusters together in a bottom-up fashion until a termination condition holds. In contrast, the *divisive* is a top-down approach that starts with all the objects in the same cluster. A cluster is split up into smaller clusters until a termination condition holds. Enhancements to these methods include more careful analysis of object linkages at each hierarchical partition [116] and using iterative relocation methods after the agglomerative method [285].

Density-Based
Density-based methods [87, 130] employ the notion of density in physics. These methods discover clusters by growing an initial cluster as long as the density in the neighborhood exceeds some density threshold. Given a cluster *c*, a density threshold requires each object in *c* to contain a minimum number of other objects in a predefined radius. Therefore, such methods can discover clusters of arbitrary shapes and can also be used to compute augmented clustering orderings for automatic and interactive cluster analysis [16].

Other clustering techniques include: *grid-based* methods [240, 262] which quantize the object space into a finite number of cells forming a grid structure, and then perform clustering on the grid structure; and *model-based* methods [239] which use hypotheses to model each cluster, then find the best fit to the model. There are also clustering algorithms combining different clustering techniques to cope with multiple clustering criteria [4].

Chapter 6

TEXT MINING

The data mining techniques used in knowledge discovery as described in Chapter 5 were originally designed to extract information from structured data. However, most data on the Web is unstructured, stored in documents or in non-alpha-numeric form such as images. Most is textual, found in memos, e-mail messages, or similar documents. Previously developed techniques for data mining are unsuitable for analyzing such unstructured textual information. In this chapter, we present the main ideas of knowledge discovery in textual information, which is called *text mining*.

1. WHAT IS TEXT MINING?

Text and data mining are part of the larger field of *information mining*, which more broadly reflects the wide variety of forms information may take. Text mining differs from data mining in that it handles text information. The text information has some implicit structure, though it is basically unstructured.

Text mining is increasingly important because of the enormous amount of knowledge residing in text documents. The advent of the Web has drastically increased the availability of such textual information. The volume and constantly changing character of Web-based text entails ongoing analysis. Text mining addresses these requirements by developing tools and techniques for analyzing this kind of dynamic information. Unlike information access or retrieval, which helps users find documents satisfying their information needs [23, 71], the goal of text mining is the discovery, recognition, or derivation of new information from large collections of text [126].

Web text mining refers to the process of searching through unstructured data on the Internet and deriving meaning from it. The process includes uncovering relationships in text collections and exploring them to discover new knowledge. Thus, text mining goes far beyond merely using statistical models, as is often done with text files. The main purposes of text mining are the following:

- Association discovery

- Trend discovery

- Event discovery

2.   ASSOCIATION DISCOVERY

As described in Chapter 5, mining association rules [7, 180] can be applied to discover rules of association between items in a large database of transactions. Similar work on association extraction in collections of texts has been conducted in [96, 98, 170, 220].

An objective measure of association rules of the form $X \Rightarrow Y$ is rule *support*, which represents the number of documents in a document collection that contain both X and Y. Another measuring rule is *confidence*, which assesses the percentage of documents in a document collection containing X that also contain Y. For example, an association rule discovered could be 9 (support) documents contain both "data" and "mining" with 90% (confidence) of certainty.

2.1   DEFINITION

Associations are extracted from collections of texts as follows. Consider a set of keywords $W' = \{w_1, w_2, \ldots, w_m\}$ associated with a collection of indexed documents $T = \{t_1, t_2, \ldots, t_n\}$. Each t_i is associated with a subset of W', denoted $t_i(W')$. Let $W \subseteq W'$ be a subset of keywords. The set of all documents t in T such that $W \subseteq t(W')$ will be called the *covering set* for W and denoted as $[W]$. In other words, $[W]$ is the set of documents in T such that each document in $[W]$ includes all the words in W as part of its list of keywords. Clearly, if $W \subseteq W'$, then $[W] \supseteq [W']$.

An *association rule* (or simply an *association*) is an implication of the form $W \Rightarrow w$, where $W \subseteq W'$ and $w \in W' - W$.

Given an association $R : W \Rightarrow w$, the support S of R with respect to the collection T is defined as:

$$S(R, T) = |[W \cup \{w\}]|$$

which means S is the actual number of indexed documents in T that contain all the keywords in $W \cup \{w\}$. This differs from the definition of the support given in Chapter 5, which was based on a percentage. If we followed the definition in Chapter 5, we would have defined the support for an association to be $\frac{|[W \cup \{w\}]|}{|T|}$.

The confidence C of R with respect to T is defined as:

$$C(R, T) = \frac{|[W \cup \{w\}]|}{|[W]|}$$

Thus, C is similar to the conditional probability that a text is indexed by the keyword w, if it is already being indexed by the keyword set W. For example, suppose $W = \{dog, cat\}$ and $w = pet$. If 90% of the indexed documents containing the keywords *dog* and *cat* also contain the keyword *pet*, then the confidence of $\{dog, cat\} \Rightarrow pet$ is 90%.

An association R discovered from a collection of texts T is said to satisfy support δ and confidence α if

$$S(R, T) \geq \delta \quad and \quad C(R, T) \geq \alpha$$

An association R satisfying the given support and confidence constraints is denoted by:

$$W \Rightarrow w \quad S(R, T)/C(R, T)$$

2.2 ALGORITHM FOR ASSOCIATION RULE DISCOVERY

Given a set of keywords $W' = \{w_1, w_2, \ldots, w_m\}$ and a collection of indexed documents $T = \{t_1, t_2, \ldots, t_n\}$, the extraction of associations satisfying the given support δ and confidence α can be decomposed into two subproblems [5]:

1. Find all the keyword sets with support at least equal to δ. This refers to all the keyword sets W such that $|[W]| \geq \delta$. The generated keyword sets are called *frequent sets*.

2. Discover all the association rules that satisfy the confidence constraint α using the frequent sets produced in Step 1.

Figure 6.1 illustrates the association rule generation algorithm. This algorithm is used after the frequent sets have been produced.

for each W in frequent sets {
      generate all the rules $W - \{w\} \Rightarrow \{w\}$, where $w \in W$,
      such that $\frac{\|[W]\|}{\|[W-\{w\}]\|} \geq \alpha$;
}

Figure 6.1.   Algorithm for association rules generation.

In the case where background knowledge is available for some specific domain, additional constraints can be integrated into the association generation algorithm [98]. Since association extraction is performed on indexed documents, techniques from information retrieval can be used for automated production of indexes associated with documents [229].

Association extraction experiments on the Reuter newswire document corpus were conducted in [96] using Knowledge Discovery in Texts (KDT) system. An example of their results is the association:

query: "Find all associations including *gold* and any country"
result: (gold, copper) $\Rightarrow$ Canada   [Support 5, Confidence 0.556]
           (gold, silver) $\Rightarrow$ USA   [Support 18, Confidence 0.692]
          . . .

The extraction of association rules from full text with Natural Language Processing techniques such as part-of-speech tagging [39, 72] and term extraction [74] has also been studied [97, 220].

3.   TREND DISCOVERY

Mining sequential patterns has been applied to the problem of discovering trends in database transactions [8]. Experiments related to sequential pattern discovery have also been conducted in text databases [165]. Trend discovery in text databases has also been applied to large collections of text files such as the U.S. Patent Database [259], as well as to discover shift of market interests from one product domain to another. For example, the occurrence of the word "Java" in recent articles on computers might suggest either an upward or downward trend in the popularity of the Java programming language. Thus, a trend might be recognized in a document collection by detecting sudden changes in the frequency of certain noun-phrases over a period of time.

3.1 DEFINITION

To discover trends in collections of texts, consider a set of words W, phrases P and text fields F, where

- $W = \{w_1, w_2, \ldots w_n\}$, where a word can also be denoted by (w_i).

- $P = \{p_1, p_2, \ldots p_n\}$, where $p_i = (w_1, w_2, \ldots, w_k)$ and $w_i \in W$.
  A phrase can also be denoted by $< (w_1)(w_2) \ldots (w_k) >$.

- $F = \{f_1, f_2, \ldots f_n\}$, where $f_i \subseteq W \cup P$.

Thus, a phrase is merely a sequence of words, while a text field is a set of words or phrases.

Given a set of text documents $T = \{t_1, t_2, \ldots, t_n\}$, let $t_i = \{TS_i, f_1, f_2, \ldots, f_m\}$, where TS_i denotes the *timestamp* of t_i and $f_i \in F$. By the timestamp of a document, we mean the time that the document is registered into the database.

To capture the notion of phrases for a more complex structure, the notion of *k-phrase* is used. A 1-phrase is a list of elements where each element is itself a phrase; for example, $< <(data)(mining)> <(book)> >$ denotes "data mining" and "book" occurring in a single paragraph. A k-phrase has k levels of nesting. For example, a 2-phrase could be $< <(Web)(mining)> <(book)> > < <(data) (mining)> >$ which denotes "Web mining" and "book" occurring in a different paragraph from "data mining".

3.2 TREND DISCOVERY ALGORITHM

The algorithm used to discover trends in a collection of texts has three major phases:

1. Identify frequent phrases.

2. Generate histories of phrases.

3. Find patterns that match a specified trend.

3.2.1   IDENTIFYING PHRASES

The phrase-identification problem (PIP) can be reduced to the problem of mining sequential patterns (MSP) [8].   The input to the MSP problem is a set of sequences, called data-sequences, where each sequence is a list of transactions. A sequence can be denoted by $S_i = < t_1, t_2, \ldots, t_n >$, where t_i is a transaction. Each transaction in turn represents a set of items, which are called elements of the pattern, and are denoted by $t_i = \{i_1, i_2, \ldots, i_n\}$. Without loss of generality, an item can be mapped to an integer. For example, <{1}, {2 3}, {5}> is a sequence with three transactions, namely, {1}, {2 3} and {5}. Each transaction has a timestamp associated with it. A *sequential pattern* is a set of items (or transactions) ordered according to their timestamp. The *support* of a sequential pattern is the percentage of data-sequences that contain the pattern. The MSP problem is to find all sequential patterns with their support greater than a user-specified minimum support. Since transactions have timestamps associated with them, the problem has been extended and generalized in [251] to include time constraints. Time constraints are used to specify a minimum and/or maximum time period between adjacent elements in a pattern. These generalizations allow items in a transaction of a sequential pattern to be present in a set of transactions whose timestamps are within a user-specified time period rather than a single transaction.

In order to solve a PIP using MSP, we need to map each word in a text to an item in a data-sequence. Appropriate nesting using parentheses must be preserved to separate words in a sentence, sentences in a paragraph, paragraphs in a section, etc. This mapping method allows the algorithm to take advantage of the structure of a document to obtain a richer set of phrases. The timestamp for each word can be defined as the order of occurrences of the word relative to the location in the document.

Distance constraints can be used to specify a minimum and/or maximum gap between adjacent words of a phrase, allowing the user to specify whether a phrase can span a sentence or paragraph.

3.2.2   PHRASE GENERATION

Documents can be partitioned based on their timestamps in order to generate histories. The granularity of the partitioning is user-specified and can be year, month or day depending on the application. For each partition there is a set of frequent phrases, found using the method defined in the previous subsection.

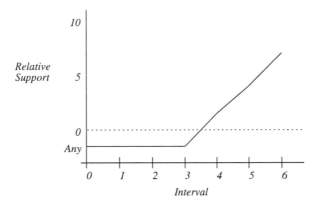

Figure 6.2. An uptrend shape query.

The result of applying MSP to a set of frequent phrases is a history of support values for each phrase which can be used to determine the trend.

3.2.3 TREND DISCOVERY

To identify a trend from a set of histories discovered for each supported k-phrase in the history generating phase, one can specify a specific shape in the histories. A language was proposed in [8], called shape definition language (SDL), to define a specific trend shape with or without support.

Trends are those k-phrases retrieved by a shape query, with constraints like the time period during which the trend is supported. Taken from [165], Figure 6.2 shows an uptrend shape query. Its corresponding SDL query is:

```
(shape strongUp () (comp Bigup Bigup Bigup))
(file "input_file")
(query (window 1) ((strongUp) (support 2 end)))
(quit)
```

4. EVENT DETECTION

News events are constantly occurring and are broadcast to billions of people around the world by news agencies such as CNN and Reuters. Broadcasting may be through radio, TV, or by transmission in the form of documents through both wired and wireless channels. These stories may then be archived by news agencies in chronological order as plain text or in an structured format such as SGML. As the volume of electronically available information increases, it becomes interesting to pay attention to newly generated news events.

The query-driven retrieval used in databases and information retrieval systems is content-based. A query specifies an object of interest by content-based characterization but it does not address such general inquiries as: What is new? This has led to the study and development of so-called "topic detection and tracking" (TDT) methods, such as k-nearest neighbor classification, Rocchio, relevance-based filtering, and benchmark evaluations [11, 100, 278].

4.1   DEFINITION

Event detection, in the context of news, is the identification of stories in continuous news streams that correspond to new or previously unidentified events. News event detection consists of two tasks: *retrospective detection* and *on-line detection.*

Retrospective detection is the process of discovering previously unidentified events in a cumulative news collection. By contrast, on-line detection is the process of identifying new events in realtime from live news feeds. Both processes are assumed to have no knowledge of the nature of the news stories, but do have access to unprocessed historical news stories, in chronological order, which they use as contrast sets. Thus news event detection is a discovery problem that mines data streams for undiscovered patterns in news story content.

News stories occur continuously, tending to come in bursts called *news bursts.* News bursts can be pictorially illustrated using a temporal histogram, where the x-axis is time (1 to 365 days), and the y-axis is the story count per day. The histograms of two fictitious news events are illustrated in Figure 6.3.

The temporal histogram illustrates three key observations: (i) news stories related to the same event tend to be temporally close, (ii) different events are usually separated by a time gap between two news bursts, (iii) a shift in vocabulary and changes in term frequency distribution are typical of a new event, (iv) events tend to be reported within a brief time window of 1 to 4 weeks. These characteristics are taken into consideration in designing event detection algorithms based on clustering methods.

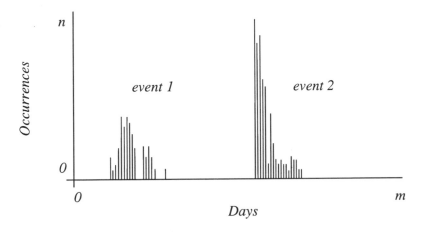

Figure 6.3.   Temporal histograms of two fictitious news events.

4.2   RETROSPECTIVE DETECTION

Retrospective detection algorithms are based on two techniques:

- detection of rapid changes in term distribution over time;

- use of the lexical similarity and proximity in time of news stories.

4.2.1   INCREMENTAL CLUSTERING

The incremental clustering method (see, e.g. [279]) is based on a vector space model [228]. It processes input documents sequentially and grows clusters incrementally. In this approach, a story is represented as a story vector whose dimensions are the stemmed unique terms (words or phrases) in the collection, and whose elements are the term weights in the story. A cluster is represented as a prototype vector that is the normalized sum of the story vectors in the cluster. Term weighting is processed after stop words, and stemming is being preprocessed. The term weighting scheme is a combination of the within-story term frequency (WSTF) and the inverse document frequency (IDF). WSTF is the number of occurrences of a term in a story. IDF provides high values for rare words and low values for common words. The weight of term τ in story δ is defined as:

$$\omega(\tau, \delta) = (1 + log_2 WSTF_{(\tau,\delta)}) \times \frac{IDF_\tau}{||\vec{\delta}||}.$$

The similarity of two stories (or clusters) is defined as the cosine value of the corresponding story vectors and prototype vectors. The following is the incremental clustering algorithm applied to each of the stories sorted in chronological order:

1. Sort the stories chronologically into a list.

2. Take the earliest story off the list and compute the cosine similarity of this story with all clusters.

3. If the highest similarity score is above a threshold, then this story is added to that cluster as a member, and the prototype vector is updated. Otherwise, this story becomes a member of a new cluster.

4. Repeat Steps 2-3 until the list is empty.

In addition to using WSTF and IDF, words and noun phrases that occur often in the collection, but not in a separate training set, can be used as potential triggers for clusters [12]. Each candidate trigger term is then examined whether or not its concentration is within a time range. If not, the term does not trigger an event. Documents that contain the triggered terms are added to a relevance feedback algorithm and a query representing an event is created to find documents that match the event. The algorithm will keep stories within a range of days by removing old stories.

4.2.2   GROUP AVERAGE CLUSTERING

Another clustering method [279] is based on modified group average clustering (GAC) algorithm [224, 271]. The method is an agglomerative algorithm that maximizes average pairwise document similarity within each cluster (note that a document is a story). It uses a vector space model [228] to represent documents and clusters, producing a binary tree of clusters in a bottom-up fashion. A straight forward GAC algorithm has time and space complexity quadratic in the number of input documents. An iterative bottom-up algorithm that trades off quality for efficiency is introduced in [73]. The following is a modified GAC clustering algorithm:

1. Sort stories in chronological order, providing an initial partition where each cluster corresponds to a single story.

2. Divide the partition into non-overlapping, consecutive buckets where each bucket contains a fixed number of clusters.

3. Apply GAC to each bucket until the number of clusters in the bucket is reduced by a factor of α.

4. Remove the bucket boundaries, while keeping clusters in chronological order.

5. Repeat Steps 2-4 until the total number of clusters is less than β.

6. After every ρ iterations of Steps 2-5, re-cluster each cluster.

This algorithm is more efficient with a time complexity of $O(mn)$, where n is the number of documents, m is the bucket size, and $m \leq n$. Step 6 is a re-clustering step added to the GAC algorithm to prevent stories belonging to the same event from being placed under different buckets.

4.3   ON-LINE DETECTION

An on-line news event detection algorithm processes stories from a news stream, one at a time, as they arrive. The output of the algorithm is a YES/NO decision based on some similarity measure with respect to previously processed news event clusters. Most on-line detection algorithms are based on a thresholding model that uses the following parameters:

- *Detection threshold t_d* – specifies the minimum similarity score required for the system to be confident that the current story belongs to a new event.

- *Clustering threshold t_c* – specifies the minimum similarity score required for the system to be willing to add the current story as a new member to an existing cluster.

- *Window size t_w* – specifies the maximum number of clusters (or other aging limits) available to compare the current story with.

The parameters are adjustable and $t_c \geq t_d$ is usually imposed to ensure better performance. A typical on-line detection algorithm has the following steps:

1. Start with an empty set of clusters K and predetermined values for t_d, t_c, and t_w, where $|K| \leq t_w$.

2. Read in a story as *current* and compute its similarity scores. Let $S = \{s_1, \ldots, s_n\}$ denote the similarity score set; here $s_i \in S$ denotes the similarity score of *current* and cluster k_i, where $k_i \in K$ and $n = |K|$.

3. Let $s_m = max\{s_1, \ldots, s_n\}$ and use the following on-line detection rules:

   (a) If $s_m \geq t_d$, then make *current* an old event (NO); otherwise, make *current* a new event (YES).

   (b) If $s_m \geq t_c$, then add *current* to cluster k_m and update the prototype vector of the cluster; otherwise, make *current* a new cluster in K. Remove the oldest cluster in K if $|K| \geq t_w$.

4. Repeat Steps 2-3 until there is no more input.

Other techniques include using k-means clustering algorithms based on "distance", or using decaying weights instead of uniformly-weighted windows to limit cluster duration time.

Chapter 7

WEB MINING

Data mining and knowledge discovery in large collections of data are known to be effective and useful as discussed in Chapter 5. With the growth of online data on the Web, the opportunity has arisen to utilize data mining techniques to analyze data stored on Web servers across the Internet. The application of data mining techniques to Web data, called *Web mining*, is used to discover patterns in this sea of information. Web mining is an evolutionary step beyond merely resource discovery and information extraction already supported by Web information retrieval systems such as the search engines and directories described in Chapter 1. In this chapter, we explore different ways for performing Web mining.

1. WHAT IS WEB MINING?

As mentioned above, Web mining is the process of applying data mining techniques to the pattern discovery in Web data. The term Web mining is generally used in three ways [105, 252]:

- Web content mining – automatic discovery of Web document content patterns.

- Web usage mining – automatic discovery of Web server access patterns.

- Web structure mining – automatic discovery of hypertext/linking structure patterns.

Web content mining is the process of analyzing text and graphic contents on the Web. It has roots in information retrieval and natural language processing. Previously unknown or hidden patterns can be extracted using this process. Text content mining is similar to the text mining discussed in Chapter 6 and graphics content mining is similar to the content-based retrieval discussed in Chapter 4.

Web usage mining is the process of analyzing Web access information available on Web servers, and consists of the automatic discovery of user access patterns from the large collections of access logs, which are daily generated by Web servers. Analyzing such data can help organizations study customers' Web browsing patterns to facilitate e-commerce specific processing such as the following:

- Web structure management – for designing a better Website.

- Promotional campaigns – for building customized advertisements.

- Marketing decisions – for making better strategic decisions.

Web structure mining is the process of analyzing the structured information used to describe Web content. Structured information on the Web can be broadly classified as *intra-page* or *inter-page*.   Inter-page structure information can be analyzed by traversing hyperlinks, and is often called Web linking structure. It is a rich source of information about the nature of the Web. In this type of mining, the linking structure can be represented as a graph in which Web documents are the nodes and hyperlinks are the directed edges of the graph. Useful information can be discovered by processing the relationships between nodes and edges. Figure 7.1 shows five basic hyperlink relationships.

Intra-page structure information refers to the internal document structure of the actual Web document in HTML or XML, which is usually represented as a tree. Mining intra-page structure is critical to extracting important information, such as schemas, for mediators and data warehouses.

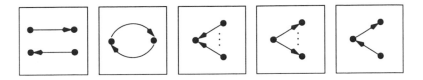

Figure 7.1. Hyperlink relationships.

In this chapter we will discuss the current state of research on Web usage mining and Web structure mining. Text-based Web content mining can be found in Chapter 1, and multimedia Web content mining can be found in Chapter 4.

2. WEB USAGE MINING

Web usage information captures activities from online users and exhibits a wide range of different behavioral patterns. The behavioral patterns can shed light on user browsing preferences, online customer behavior and future Website improvement directions.

There are a number of issues in mining Web access logs, which arise from the characteristics of the client-server model for the Web. In this section, we will discuss four processing stages of Web usage mining: usage data collection, usage data preprocessing, usage pattern discovery, and usage pattern analysis.

2.1 WEB USAGE DATA COLLECTION

Web usage data collected from different sources reflects the different types of usage tracking appropriate for different purposes. Usage information can be collected from the following sources:

- Web server – stores access logs to the server.

- Web proxy server – stores access logs from anonymous users sharing the same proxy server.

- Client machine – stores browsing logs on the client side.

2.1.1 WEB SERVER LOG DATA

Web servers store access request information in Web server access logs. Access logs are like fingerprints characterizing Web servers. For each browsing session to a Web server, entries are recorded in the following log files:

- Access logs – store client access information.

- Error logs – store failure client access information.

- Cookie logs – store session information between client and server.

Access logs store such access information as the date, client IP, request URL, bytes transferred, etc. The storing format is either common log or extended log. Pages cached by proxy servers and information passed through the POST method are not recorded in log files, but these limitations can be handled by using packet sniffers to directly extract usage data from TCP/IP packets.

On a heavily used Website, multiple servers may be deployed to handle requests in a round-robin fashion for load balancing. One problem with this type of Website configuration is that a user's browsing session logs can be scattered across different servers. In this case, logs from different servers must be gathered.

Another problem is that although a log entry is added for each page request that reaches the Web server, this does not necessarily reflect all the requests made to the site. For example, a proxy server frequently caches requested pages and returns them to a requesting client without notifying the Web server. In this case, logs in the Web server under-represent the actual usage, which could only be obtained by including logs from proxy servers.

Error logs store failure information from request attempts made by clients. Common failures include missing links, authentication failures, timeout problems, server errors, implementation errors, bad requests, methods not allowed, etc. A complete list of error codes is defined in the HTTP/1.0 and HTTP/1.1 specification [273].

Cookie logs store cookies (special client side data), which are used in keeping track of access sessions made by possibly different users from the same host. Cookies are generated by the Web server and held by the clients to keep track of browsing states. However, cookies rely on implicit user cooperation to allow the Web browser to store them on a client machine.

Although these different types of logs are constantly updated by the Web servers in the course of capturing daily Web usage information, access logs contain the most interesting patterns waiting to be discovered. Commercial access log analysis products such as those described in [131, 171, 204] emphasize statistical access analysis. This provides limited support for reporting user activity and is inadequate for more sophisticated types of analyses.

Earlier research work on access logs includes [58], which introduced the notion of maximal forward references to break down user sessions into transactions. [179] used server logs to discover frequent episodes. [277] partitioned site visitors in clusters. Pattern discovery is addressed in more recent studies in [42, 66, 67, 142, 196, 202, 238, 246, 247, 252, 280, 283].

2.1.2 WEB PROXY SERVER LOG DATA

Proxy server logs may be used as data sources for characterizing the browsing behavior of users sharing common proxy servers. A Web proxy server acts as a gateway between internal and external networks. It deals with two types of requests: external servers on behalf of internal clients and internal servers on behalf of external clients. A proxy server usually resides in a firewall, which restricts access to a protected network. Proxy caching software, like Squid [248] and the Apache [17] proxy module, is often used to reduce the loading time and network traffic on a Website. HTTP requests are intercepted without being forwarded to the Web server due to the caching mechanism. This makes proxy traces a good data source for mining useful patterns in combination with Web server logs. However, it has been observed that local caching and proxy servers are the two biggest impediments to collecting reliable usage data [217].

2.1.3 CLIENT MACHINE LOG DATA

Client machine log data resides on the client side. It is undoubtedly the best source of data for revealing a client's browsing patterns, and mitigates both caching and session identification problems. Client-side data collection can be achieved by using remote agents implemented in JavaScripts or as Java applets, or by modifying the source code of an existing open source browser such as Mozilla [197]. User cooperation is required to enable the functionality of the JavaScripts and Java applets, or to use modified browsers. Data collected by modified browsers is more versatile because the JavaScripts and Java applets have limited data collection abilities.

2.2 USAGE DATA PREPROCESSING

A Web server access log contains records of user accesses. Each entry in the log represents a page request from a client on the Internet. This log must be obtained from the Web server in order to find patterns in it.

Usage logs are stored as text files under a specified directory on the Web server. Logs are generated using the common logfile format specified as part of the HTTP protocol by CERN and NCSA [273] that many Web servers use. This format is as follows:

```
remotehost rfc931 authuser [date] "request" status bytes
```

- `remotehost` - Remote hostname or IP number.

- `rfc931` - The remote logname of the user.

- `authuser` - The username under which the user has authenticated himself.

- `[date]` - Date and time of the request.

- `"request"` - The request line exactly as it came from the client.

- `status` - The HTTP status code returned to the client.

- `bytes` - The content-length of the document transferred to the client.

A typical entry from the Apache Web server [17] access log looks like:

```
www.sample.org - - [15/Apr/2000:00:03:24 -0400]
"GET /index.html HTTP/1.0" 200 11371
```

User activities are categorized by the W3C Web characterization activity (WCA) [263] as follows:

- Page view – visual rendering of a Web page in a specific client environment at a specific point in time.

- Click stream – a set of user-initiated requests which can be either explicit, implicit, embedded, or user clicks.

- Server session – a collection of user clicks to a single Web server during a user session (also called a visit).

- User session – a delimited set of user clicks across one or more Web servers.

- Episode – a subset of related user clicks that occur within a user session.

Logs from different sources are sorted according to the [date] field. The data preparation stage cleans data by applying methods such as path name completion and filename suffixes conversion, filters irrelevant data items such as sound and image access entries, identifies different visitors, and groups accesses into different session units (transactions).

2.3 USAGE PATTERN DISCOVERY

Different types of data use different pattern discovery techniques. The discovered knowledge is then used to perform tasks such as customization, prediction, and enhancing existing Website infrastructure. The following is a list of data mining techniques that have been applied to Web usage data.

Statistical Analysis
Statistical analysis is the most commonly used method to extract and report information about site visitors. Many log analysis tools use this technique to analyze site traffic including frequently accessed pages, average file size, daily traffic, the number of site visitors, access error reporting, etc. The discovery of facts about a Website is potentially useful for monitoring usage, security checking, performance tuning, and site improvement.

Association Rule Discovery
The discovery of association rules in a usage log refers to the identification of sets of pages accessed together with a support value exceeding a predefined threshold value. The discovered rules represent knowledge about user's access behavior, which has significance in both business and site enhancing values. For example, marketing people can use the discovered rules for marketing applications while Webmasters can use them for site restructuring.

Clustering

Clustering is used when categories are unknown. Therefore, it can be used in the Web usage domain to group similar Web-related data items. Two interesting types of Web data to which to apply clustering techniques are user sessions and accessed pages. Both provide insight into user browsing behavior. For example, in clustering user sessions, customers having a similar browsing pattern are grouped together.

Classification

Classification is used when categories are defined. Given a user's browsing pattern, a classification technique can be used to classify this user into different categories of interests. Large classification tasks can lead to the discovery of hidden patterns, which would be otherwise unnoticed.

Sequential Pattern Discovery

Sequential pattern discovery applied to usage logs refers to the mining of frequently occurring patterns in user sessions or episodes. For example, certain users might access certain pages with periodicity. Periodic patterns can be discovered through this type of analysis, which is useful in discovering trends in databases.

2.4   USAGE PATTERN ANALYSIS

Pattern analysis is the last phase in the Web usage mining process. This process filters uninteresting rules or patterns from the set of discovered patterns gathered in the pattern discovery phase. One approach is to construct a Web log data cube and apply OLAP operations as described in Chapter 5. The most common filtering tools are based on query languages such as DMQL [119], MINE RULE [188], MSQL [135], M*i*DAS [41], and WUM [27].

3.   WEB STRUCTURE MINING

The Web structure represented by hyperlinks in hypertext is a rich source for pattern discovery. The structure at large contains a considerable amount of undiscovered information to be analyzed. With millions of links on the Web, individuals can impose linking structures at local levels, which leaves the global organization unplanned. Thus, an understanding of high-level structures can emerge only through a posterior analysis. This type of analysis is also called connectivity or link topology analysis.

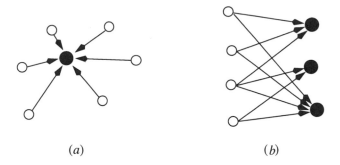

(a)   (b)

Figure 7.2.   Hubs and authorities.

In [148], a hyperlink-induced topic search (HITS) algorithm was developed for analyzing hyperlink topology by discovering authoritative information
sources for a broad search topic. So-called hyperlinked communities can be
discovered using this framework [101, 106, 152]. The discovery of two inter-
related types of pages called *authorities* and *hubs* is the central focus of this
work.

HITS is simple and mathematically clean and has been extended and improved in algorithms developed in [34, 51, 52], and [216] uses textual similarity
and link structure to identify major topical themes. Citation analysis [270] on
the Web topology similar to HITS is also studied in [158, 210] and is the technique powering the Google search engine [114] and the Clever system [50, 63].

3.1   HUBS AND AUTHORITIES

Denote a link from page ρ to page δ as $\rho \rightarrow \delta$. Such links encode considerable
latent human judgment when embedded in a document by its creator. The link
confirms not only the importance of document δ to ρ, but also its relevance to
ρ. Thus, authorities can be viewed as highly-referenced pages on a specific
topic, as illustrated by the black node in Figure 7.2(a). Hubs can be defined as
pages that link to many related authorities, as illustrated by the white nodes in
Figure 7.2(b).

Authorities and hubs exhibit strong mutually reinforcing relationships because a hub becomes a better hub when it links to many good authorities.

Likewise, an authority becomes a better authority when it is linked to many good hubs. This type of analysis is called *connectivity analysis.*

3.2   CONNECTIVITY ANALYSIS

Connectivity analysis can be used to discover topic or query specific communities by computing the hubs and authorities for the topic. Finding communities is related to the NP-complete graph partitioning problem, but properties of hypertext turn it into a source-sink maximum flow network problem, which has many polynomial time solutions [101]. The basic algorithm requires the following four steps:

1. Given a query or topic Q, a root-set $S = \{s_1, \ldots, s_n\}$ of n seed pages is collected by making a search request, based on Q, to a search engine. Typically, only a fixed number of the pages returned by the search engine should be used.

2. The root-set S is then expanded to a larger set T, called a base set or neighborhood graph, by adding any page p that has a hyperlink to/or from any page in S. That is, $T = S \cup N$, where $N = \{\rho \mid \exists \delta \in S$ such that either $\rho \to \delta$ or $\delta \to \rho\}$. The relationship between T and S is depicted in Figure 7.3.

3. Each page $\rho \in T$ is initially assigned an authority weight and a hub weight of 1, denoted by $\alpha(\rho)$ and $\lambda(\rho)$, respectively. Each page's λ and α are then iteratively updated as follows:

$$\alpha(\rho) = \sum_{\delta \to \rho} \lambda(\delta),$$

$$\lambda(\rho) = \sum_{\rho \to \delta} \alpha(\delta).$$

Thus, each iteration replaces $\alpha(\rho)$ by the sum of $\lambda(\delta)$, where δ links to ρ; and then replaces $\lambda(\rho)$ by the sum of $\alpha(\delta)$, where ρ links to δ. Normalize $\lambda(\rho)$ and $\alpha(\rho)$ and repeat Step 3 until λ and α converge to stable sets of hub and authority weights, which typically takes about 10 iterations.

4. The community is discovered by taking the top k pages with the highest α value and the top k pages with the highest λ value.

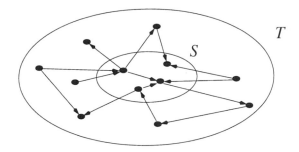

Figure 7.3. Root-set and base set.

The process of expanding a root-set S to a larger set T in step 2 requires obtaining inlinks and outlinks to nodes in S. Inlinks are hyperlinks that link to S and outlinks are hyperlinks that link from S. Inlinks can be gathered by using queries of the form *link: url* in the AltaVista [13] search engine. This query form returns a list of URLs that link to *url*. Fast access to hypertext linkage information is provided by the Connectivity Server [33], which is built on pages indexed by the AltaVista search engine.

3.3 CONNECTIVITY ANALYSIS WITH WEIGHTS

The connectivity analysis algorithm discussed in the previous subsection does not guarantee finding all important hubs and authorities because there may be relevant pages on the Web with good content that have neither been linked to nor referenced by these pages. Three additional cases in which the method described in the previous subsection tends to fail include [34]:

- falsely identified authorities and hubs,

- falsely established links created by automated tools, and

- falsely identified relevant nodes.

Pages can be misidentified as authorities and hubs when links referenced by or to the same page/host unfairly drive up both hub and authority scores, due to the mutually reinforcing nature of hubs and authorities, under the influence of a single page/host. This problem can be solved by assigning fractional weights to indegree or outdegree edges as introduced in [34]. Given a page ρ, an indegree edge respect to ρ is an edge that links to ρ, and an outdegree edge is an edge that links from ρ. An indegree edge is assigned an authority weight of $\frac{1}{j}$ if there are j edges with the same endpoint from documents on the same host. An outdegree edge is assigned a hub weight of $\frac{1}{k}$ if there are k edges from the same document to a set of documents on the same host. These fractional multipliers are called the authority fractional weighting factor (AFWF) and hub fractional weighting factor (HFWF), respectively. The modified formulas for Step 3 in the method described in the previous subsection are as follow:

$$\alpha(\rho) = \sum_{\delta \to \rho} \lambda(\delta) \times AFWF(\rho, \delta),$$

$$\lambda(\rho) = \sum_{\rho \to \delta} \alpha(\delta) \times HFWF(\delta, \rho).$$

3.4   CONNECTIVITY ANALYSIS WITH DISTANCE

Association of Web pages using connectivity analysis is further extended in [260] using the hypothesis that associations of Web pages are induced by the connectivity and path length factors described below:

- Connectivity factor – the fact that two pages appear on more paths is considered as a stronger indication of why these two pages are associated.

- Path length factor – pages on shorter paths have a stronger association than those on longer paths.

To address the associativity problem introduced by paths, we my consider the distance between pages. Let v_i and v_j denote Web pages, and p_u denote a path, with length $|p_u|$. $v_i \overset{p_u}{\leadsto} v_j$ represents p_u is from v_i to v_j. Let $S = \{s_1, \ldots, s_n\}$ denote a set of Web pages, called a root-set. Given a distance d, the task of connectivity analysis based on the distance among S is to find a set of pages $S' = \{s'_1, \ldots, s'_m\}$ that best induces the association in S. This is described as: $\forall s'_i \in S', \exists s_j \in S$ such that $s_j \overset{p_q}{\leadsto} s'_i \vee s'_i \overset{p_u}{\leadsto} s_j$ where $|p_q|$ and $|p_u| \leq d$.

Based on the distance, pages with high connectivity but far away from the root-set may be less significant than those pages that have low connectivity but are close to the root-set. Pages that satisfy both factors would be considered a good representative for the association.

Chapter 8

WEB CRAWLING AGENTS

An essential component of information mining and pattern discovery on the Web is the Web Crawling Agent (WCA). General-purpose Web Crawling Agents, which were briefly described in Chapter 1, are intended to be used for building generic portals. The diverse and voluminous nature of Web documents presents formidable challenges to the design of high performance WCAs. They require both powerful processors and a tremendous amount of storage, and yet even then can only cover restricted portions of the Web. Nonetheless, despite their fundamental importance in providing Web services, the design of WCAs is not well-documented in the literature. This chapter describes the conceptual design and implementation of Web crawling agents.

1.   WHAT IS A WEB CRAWLING AGENT?

The term "Web crawling agent" combines the concepts of *agent* and *Web crawler*. Web crawling agents are responsible for intelligently gathering important data from the Web, data which can then be used in a pattern discovery process.

1.1   WHAT IS AN AGENT?

The term "agent" is used in different ways in contemporary computing, the following three being the most common:

- Autonomous agents – refer to self-maintained programs that can move between hosts according to conditions in the environment.

- Intelligent agents – refer to programs that assist users in finding requested data items, filling forms, and using software.

- User-agents – refer to programs that execute requests for services through a network on behalf of a user. For example, Netscape Navigator is a Web user-agent and Eudora is an email user-agent.

Autonomous agents can travel only between special hosts for security reasons and are not widely used on the Internet. Intelligent agents are host-based software that have little to do with networking. User-agents need constant interaction and have limited intelligence. Web crawling agents exhibit the characteristics of both intelligent agents and user-agents, since they act intelligently and sometimes require user interaction. However, they are not autonomous agents since they do not travel between hosts.

1.2   WHAT IS A WEB CRAWLER?

Web crawlers, which were briefly discussed in Chapter 1, are also known as crawlers, robots, spiders, walkers, wanderers, and worms. The Web crawlers are responsible for gathering resources from the Web, such as HTML documents, images, postscript files, text files and news postings. Due to the large volume of data on the Web, there is a need to automate the resource gathering process, which motivates the use of Web crawlers.

In general, crawlers are programs that automatically traverse the Web via hyperlinks embedded in hypertext, news group listings, directory structures or database schemas. In contrast, browsers are utilized by a user to interactively traverse portions of the Web by following hyperlinks explicitly selected by the user or by interfacing with search engines sites. Crawlers are commonly used by search engines to generate their indexes [215]. The traversal methods used by crawlers include depth-first and breadth-first search combined with heuristics that determine the order in which to visit documents. An empirical study conducted in [162] has shown that roughly 190 million Web pages have been indexed by six major search engines. More recently, Google announced that its index encompasses over one billion (10^9) pages. All of these indexed pages were visited by crawlers deployed by the search engines.

Early papers on Web crawling include [84, 181, 215]; more recent studies are [53, 59, 129, 257]. According to the literature, crawlers are used to perform the following tasks:

- Indexing – build and maintain indexes for search engines.

- HTML validation – check whether a page conforms to HTML DTD.

- Link validation – check whether a link is still valid.

- Information monitoring – monitor changes to HTML pages.

- Information search – search for wanted documents.

- Mirroring – build mirror (duplicate) sites.

2.   WEB CRAWLING ARCHITECTURE

Designing a scalable and extensible Web crawling agent presents formidable challenges due to the large volume of data on the Web. By *scalable*, we mean the crawling agent must be able to scale up to the entire Web. The design of scalable crawling agents presents both software and hardware challenges since system hardware must be able to sustain constant heavy loads from the streams of data retrieved by the crawling agents. On the *extensible* side, the system must be designed in a modular way. The support for extensibility and customizability must be easily achieved by plugging in third party software or hardware modules.

The architecture of a Web crawling agent consists of the following subsystems:

- Retrieving Module

- Processing Module

- Formatting Module

- URL Listing Module

Web crawling systems use multiple processors to share the load of information gathering and processing. A scalable distributed Web crawling system can effectively utilize these computing resources by using collaborative Web crawling [257]. Figure 8.1 illustrates the architecture of a distributed Web crawling system. The components used in this system are described below.

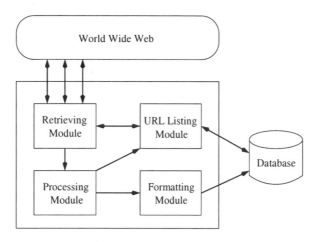

Figure 8.1.   A Web crawling architecture.

2.1   RETRIEVING MODULE

The Retrieving Module is responsible for retrieving all types of information in any format (text, image, graphics, audio, video) from the Web. The
Retrieving Module fetches URLs from a pool of candidate URLs stored in
the URL Listing Module. The Retrieving Module can be implemented using prebuilt components in various languages. Figure 8.2 illustrates a simple
Retrieving Module written in Perl which retrieves an HTML page. It uses
the Libwww-Perl library, a collection of Perl modules that provides a simple,
consistent programming interface to the World Wide Web. For additional information on Perl, refer to Comprehensive Perl Archive Network (CPAN) at
http://www.perl.com/CPAN/.

The program in Figure 8.2 uses three Perl modules: URI, HTTP, and LWP.
First, a URL in the URI module is initialized with http://www.kluwer.nl,
followed by instantiation of a UserAgent in the LWP module. The request is then
prepared using the HTTP GET method and requested using the UserAgent's
request method. If the response is successful and the returned content type
is HTML, then the page content is displayed; otherwise, an error message is
displayed.

Due to the latency effects caused by network traffic and server load, the
Retrieving Module should be designed to allow simultaneous requests to mul-

```perl
#!/usr/bin/perl
use URI::URL;
use HTTP::Request;
use HTTP::Response;
use LWP::UserAgent;

my $request_url = "http://www.kluwer.nl";
my $html_page = new URI::URL($request_url);
my $agent = new LWP::UserAgent;
my $request = new HTTP::Request('GET', $html_page);
my $response = $agent->request($request);

if ($response->is_success &&
    $response->header('Content-type') eq 'text/html') {
    print $response->content;
} else {
    print "ERROR: $request_url failed!\n";
}
```

Figure 8.2.   A simple Retrieving Module.

tiple Web servers. Sites like Google and Internet Archive use multiple machines for crawling [40, 46]. Retrieved resources are then passed to the Processing Module.

2.2   PROCESSING MODULE

The Processing Module is responsible for processing retrieved resources. Its functions include (i) determining the retrieved data type, (ii) summary extraction, (iii) hyperlink extraction, and (iv) interaction with knowledge bases or databases. The result is then passed to the Formatting Module. The Processing Module must also be capable of making decisions as to which URLs should be added to the pool of candidate URLs stored in the URL Listing Module.

2.3   FORMATTING MODULE

The Formatting Module is responsible for converting the diverse types of data sources retrieved and for transforming or summarizing them into a uniform metadata format. The metadata format generally reflects the format that will be used in the pattern discovery phase, and includes tuples that can be inserted into database tables and XML documents.

2.4   URL LISTING MODULE

The URL Listing Module is responsible for feeding the Retrieving Module with candidate URLs to be retrieved. Usually a pool of candidates is stored in a queue with first-come-first-serve priority scheduling, unless specified otherwise. This module can also insert new candidate URLs into its list from the Processing Module.

3.   CRAWLING ALGORITHMS

A crawling agent uses an algorithm, often called a crawling algorithm, to retrieve Web pages and files. For example, in Harvest [36], the crawling algorithm starts by retrieving an initial page, P_0, or a set of initial pages, $\{P_0 \ldots P_n\}$. The initial pages(s) are pre–selected by the user. URLs are extracted from the retrieved pages and added to a queue of URLs to be processed. The crawler then gets URLs from the queue and repeats the process.

One of the main objectives of a search engine is to capture the most recent view of the Web that can be achieved. However, most crawlers will not be able to visit every possible page for the following reasons:

- In addition to scanning the Web for new pages, a crawler must also periodically revisit pages already seen to update changes made since the last visit. These changes affect the index and crawling paths.

- Server resources are limited by their storage capacity. The Web has been estimated to contain 320 million indexable pages [162] and has already grown provably beyond one billion (10^9) pages [137].

- Network bandwidth is limited to the type and number of connections to the Internet. Only a limited number of simultaneous crawlers can be launched by a given Web crawling system.

Due to these limitations, smart crawling techniques are needed to capture the most current view of the Web in the most efficient manner. Two recent studies on smart crawling techniques propose crawling using techniques called URL ordering [59] and collaborative Web crawling [257]. These techniques significantly improve the efficiency and accuracy of crawlers.

3.1   URL ORDERING

Let $V = \{p_x, \ldots, p_y\}$ be a set of visited pages and $U = \{p_m, \ldots, p_n\}$ be a set of pages, called *front pages*, defined as follows:

1. U consists of unvisited pages only, so U and V are disjoint.

2. For all $p_i \in U$, there exists a $p_j \in V$, such that p_i is 1-distance away from p_j (i.e., every page in U is at most one link away from a page in V). Since hyperlinks are directed paths, the converse may not hold.

Figure 8.3 illustrates the concept of front pages. The visited pages are the white nodes and front pages are the black nodes.

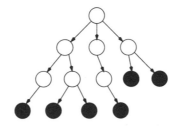

Figure 8.3.   Illustration of front pages.

Front pages are stored in a queue in order of visitation, and await processing by the crawler. At any given instant in the crawling process, the decision according to which a crawler selects a page p_i from this pool of front pages is important. Selecting the most important pages to visit is significant because we want to maximize the crawler's ability to find the most important pages on the Web. Several useful definitions of this importance measure can be used to prioritize the crawling order of front pages.

Given a Web page p_i, an importance measure of this page can be defined using one or a combination of the following methods:

- Document similarity measure

- hyperlink measure

- URL measure

Different implementation measures yield different URL orderings for crawling. The more important a page is, the earlier it is visited by the crawler. We describe each importance measure in turn below.

3.1.1   DOCUMENT SIMILARITY MEASURE

The similarity between a pair of pages is one indication of their mutual relevance. For example, pages containing many of the same keywords would presumably be relevant to each other. Relevance is in turn an indicator of importance.

In a document similarity measure method, $sim(P,Q)$ is defined as the textual similarity between P and Q, where P is a Web page and Q is the query used as the search criterion that drives the crawler. For example, the criterion can be "Find all documents related to data mining". To compute similarities, a vector model [230] developed for information retrieval can be used. Basically, P and Q are represented as t-dimensional vectors, where t is the total number of index terms in the system. The degree of similarity of P and Q is the correlation between the vectors $\vec{P}$ and $\vec{Q}$. This correlation can be quantified by using the cosine of the angle between these two vectors as follows:

$$sim(P,Q) = \frac{\vec{P} \bullet \vec{Q}}{|\vec{P}| |\vec{Q}|}$$

Thus, if the vectors are identical, the similarity is one. On the other hand, if the vectors have no terms in common (i.e. they are orthogonal), the similarity is zero.

Dissimilarity can be measured by the inverse document frequency (IDF) of a term w_i in the page collection. IDF is used to distinguish a relevant document from a non–relevant one by the number of times the term w_i occurs in a page. Observe that frequently occurring terms are not helpful in this decision process. Furthermore, because the crawler has not visited all pages, the IDF can only be calculated from the visited pages.

Other document similarity models such as the Boolean, probabilistic, and fuzzy set models can also be used.

3.1.2   HYPERLINK MEASURE

Given a Web page, P, there are two types of links with respect to P (c.f. Section 3.2 in Chapter 7):

- Back-links or inlinks – which are hyperlinks that are linked to P.

- Forward-links or outlinks – which are hyperlinks that are linked from P.

The *back-link count* is defined as the number of back-links to P; the *forward-link count* is defined as the number of forward-links from P.

The assumption underlying the use of this measure is that a page is important if there are many back-links to it. The corresponding importance measure $\zeta(P)$ is defined as the number of links to P over the entire Web. A crawler may estimate $\zeta(P)$ based on the number of back-links to P from pages it has visited or using search engines to get pre-calculated back-link counts.

The forward-link count for a page P is not an indicator of whether P is an important page. Furthermore, links to a page should be weighted differently if they are from an important site such as the homepage of a major search engine. This idea leads to the development of a page rank metric [210] which calculates $\zeta(P)$ using the weighted value for each page: a page with many back-links from important pages should be considered important.

3.1.3   URL MEASURE

In this method, $\zeta(P)$ is a function of its hyperlink location (URL), rather than its text contents. For example, URLs ending with ".com" would have different weights than those with other endings. A URL starting with "www" and "home" may be more interesting because it represents the homepage of a Website.

3.2   WEB–GRAPH PARTITIONING

The Web is often viewed as a directed graph $G = (V, E)$, where each $v \in V$ corresponds to a Web page or URL and the hyperlinks between pages define the set E of directed edges. From a graph point of view, building a scalable, distributed collaborative Web crawling system (CWCS) [257] corresponds to developing a Web-graph partitioning algorithm for automatic load balancing among crawling processors.

How are the processors affected by graph partitioning? Ideally one wants each processor to process a disjoint set of URLs from the other processors. However, since pages are interlinked in an unpredictable way, it is not obvious how this can be done. Additionally, the processors must communicate with one another to ensure they are not redundantly processing URLs. An effective

Web graph partitioning algorithm will attempt to partition the Web-graph to minimize redundancy.

One of the main difficulties in the crawling process derives from the fact that G is unknown prior to the crawling process occurring. Furthermore, even after the crawling process is performed, only the subsets of G are known. This is because the Web is undergoing dynamic changes—information is being added and deleted, even as crawling is taking place. Moreover, not all reachable sites are visited. This complicates the application of graph partitioning methods such as those designed for static graphs in VLSI circuit design. Dynamic re-partitioning and load re-balancing are required for the Web-graph.

A *k-way* partition of the Web-graph $G = (V, E)$ is a division of G into k sub-graphs $U = (U_1, U_2, \ldots, U_k)$, where k is the number of processors in the system. Each U_i is mapped to processor i and $L_{i,j}$ denotes the set of cross partition links from U_i to U_j. The communication between processors i and j, reflected in the links in $L_{i,j}$, represents overhead in a collaborative Web crawling system.

The partitioning scheme has three basic steps:

1. *Coarsening.* Apply node and edge contraction to the Web-graph in order to obtain a manageable structure to which to apply the partitioning algorithm.

2. *Partitioning.* Apply a static graph partitioning algorithm to divide the coarsened Web-graph, and then project this partition back to the original Web-graph.

3. *Dynamic re-coarsening and repartitioning.* When the load becomes unbalanced, re-coarsen the Web-graph and repartition the coarsened Web-graph based on the current Web-graph information generated by the crawler after the last partitioning.

4.   TOPIC-ORIENTED WEB CRAWLING

The first generation of Web search engines assumed queries could be posed about any topic. This single database model of information retrieval was successful because the Web was limited in size and in the complexity of its contents [48]. Indeed, while it is true that when a query is made to a search engine, the query is most likely related to a limited set of topics [65]; nonetheless, such a "one size fits all" model of search tends to limit diversity, competition, and functionality [160]. Consequently, Web search has evolved beyond the single database model to the multi-database, topic-oriented model, in an effort to reflect the diversity of topics on the Web, as well as to achieve higher precision search results.

Topic-oriented Web crawling (TOWC) [53, 78] was designed to facilitate building topic-oriented search engines. TOWC is intended to search the portion of the Web most closely related to a specific topic. In the TOWC approach, the links in the crawling queue are reordered, as described in Section 3.1 of this chapter, to increase the likelihood that relevant pages are discovered quickly.

To achieve this, TOWC algorithms start with a seed-set (or root-set) of relevant pages as described in Section 3 of Chapter 7, and then attempt to efficiently seek out relevant documents based on a combination of link structure and page content analysis, using criteria such as: in-degree link count, out-degree link count, authority score, hub score, and topic-relevant score.

The first four criteria were discussed in Section 3 of Chapter 7. Topic-relevant scoring functions use techniques such as: *text classification* to classify and rank the relevance of a Web page to a given topic and build a topic hierarchy [83, 182]; *machine learning* to classify vectors in multi-dimensional space [223]; and *PageRank measures* to compute a weighted hyperlink measure, which is intended to be proportional to the quality of the page containing the hyperlink [40]. TOWC has been successfully used to efficiently generate indexes for search portals and user groups [183].

III

A CASE STUDY IN ENVIRONMENTAL ENGINEERING

Chapter 9

ENVIRODAEMON

1. BACKGROUND

Engineers and scientists have longed for instantaneous, distributed network access to the entire science and technology literature. These longings are well on their way to being realized as a result of the improvement and convergence of the computing and communications infrastructure and the indispensability of the Internet for scientific research. The size of the organization able to perform a search has decreased as groups of lay people and scientists can now search "digital libraries" without the aid of trained reference librarians.

Similarly, as discussed in the previous chapters, the document being sought has changed: from a citation with descriptive headers, to an abstract, to complete multimedia contents including text, audio, video, and animation. There are many reasons for the rise in digital information. The preservation of the contents of physical, paper-based texts, the convenience associated with maintaining, searching and retrieving electronic text, and the lowered cost of acquiring and maintaining electronic information as opposed to books and journals are often cited reasons [167].

This chapter reports a system for Internet search in a category-specific area: the environment. In the environmental domain, sustainable development is influenced by environmental decisions throughout the entire life-cycle of products (in a wide sense, including non-tangible products and services). In the early stages of the life-cycle, for example, in requirements gathering and design, decisions may be made with far-reaching consequences for the rest of the products' life-cycle. At this point in time, it is clearly impractical to teach all the people involved in such decisions all relevant environmental considerations. A more practical approach is to make tools available that permit those people most directly involved in the decision making to evaluate various alternatives of the products, and to assess the environmental impact of their decisions.

Such tools will rely heavily on locating relevant information, and making it available in a suitable form when it is needed. Current tools for locating information, such as the Web search engines discussed in Chapter 1, are mostly keyword based, and are not adequate for identifying relevant items and filtering out irrelevant ones. As a consequence, needed information is not easily available, and the quality of the work performed may suffer.

Searching involves queries that can involve structure (i.e., words or concepts). There are two basic types of hypertext queries: content queries, which are based on the content of a single node of the hypertext; and structure-specifying queries, which take advantage of the information, conveyed in the hypertext organization itself. Retrieval involves end user displays such as graphical user interfaces commonly, and can involve categorization, filtering and routing.

At present, access to the Web is based on navigationally oriented browsers. The end result is often a "lost-in-cyberspace" phenomenon because a) there is no reliable road map for the Web; b) obtained information is heterogeneous and difficult to analyze; and c) organization of documents conveys information which is often not exploited.

Most of the currently available Web search tools as described in Part I suffer from some of the following drawbacks:

- User partial knowledge is not fully exploited. For example, the user may know that a particular keyword is in the header or in the body of a document which would aid in its location and retrieval.

- The restructuring ability of current tools is limited or nonexistent. The querying tool should permit ad hoc specification of the format in which the answer should be presented. One should be able to search for two chapters that have references to the same article or to view two references side by side when output is given.

- The dynamic nature of Web documents are unaccounted for, which results in poor query result quality.

The primary need of end users is to quickly and easily help them find the exact piece of information they need (even though they might not be able to exactly describe their needs) without letting them drown in an information sea. When faced with the task of searching for something, one can ask for recommendations for Websites from others or use Web indexes which are manually constructed and organized by category (e.g., the search engine Yahoo! is a good example). Using this latter scheme, sites appear more quickly than can be indexed by hand and a search engine can rapidly scan an index of Web pages for certain key words. A better solution involves the use of visualization methods.

2. ENVIRODAEMON (ED)

As mentioned before, information retrieval has evolved from searches of references, to abstracts, to documents. Search on the Web involves search engines that promise to parse full-text and other files: audio, video, and multimedia. With the indexable Web approaching one billion pages and growing, difficulties with locating relevant information have become apparent. The most prevalent means for information retrieval relies on syntax-based methods: keywords or strings of characters are presented to a search engine, and it returns all the matches in the available documents. This method is satisfactory and easy to implement, but it has some inherent limitations that make it unsuitable for many tasks. Instead of looking for syntactical patterns, the user is often interested in keyword meaning or the location of a particular word in a title or header.

In this section we describe in detail a search engine developed in our lab, called EnviroDaemon. This system was built to ease the task of finding information about pollution prevention (P2), an emerging environmental field in which a premium is placed on preventing pollution in the first place instead of accepting waste as a given and treatment and disposal as necessary evils.

EnviroDaemon [124] automatically builds and updates a catalog of objects at pre-selected Internet sites that are related to P2. Users search for information by submitting keywords. Searches can be restricted to small subsets of the indexed sites by choosing one of five search criteria (Pollution Prevention and Pollution Control, Regulatory, International, ISO 14000, and Recycling and Materials Exchange), or the entire catalog can be searched. The results are returned rapidly and are embedded in several lines of text to provide context.

If the text looks promising, the user can click on a hyperlink to access the full article. Figure 9.1 shows the front-end interface for EnviroDaemon. In contrast to generic search engines such as Yahoo! and Lycos, EnviroDaemon is highly specific, focusing solely on P2 information.

EnviroDaemon employs software constructs termed **Gatherer** and **Broker** of the Harvest application system to gather, extract, organize, retrieve and filter information. Atop Harvest is the Glimpse tool, which functions as an indexer of the information and provides a query system for searching through all of the files. EnviroDaemon updates its catalog of more than 35,000 pollution prevention-related objects from about 160 Internet servers regularly.

The Internet holds vast stores of information pertaining to pollution prevention and environmental issues, and with each day more is added. Yet, as this storehouse grows, the difficulty of finding specific information increases. This section details how EnviroDaemon was built to ease the task of finding this information and building a knowledge base.

More and more of the information that environmental managers need is becoming available on the Internet. Each day, an increasing amount of valuable, substantive information is made available via sources like Websites, email list servers, and bulletin board systems. While many of these computerized information sources are potentially helpful, no organized structure exists to catalog all the data to enable someone to find specific information quickly. This is true of pollution prevention (P2), a rapidly developing field of environmental science and engineering that focuses on elimination of sources of hazardous substances, rather than on treatment or disposal.

To make computerized pollution prevention information more easily accessible, we developed EnviroDaemon, a P2-specific search engine. EnviroDaemon is designed to be useful for anyone who is searching the Internet for environmental information, whether that person is a government policymaker, consultant, researcher, student, or environmental advocate.

One can query certain specialized environmental databases (for instance, the Solvent Alternatives Guide-SAGE [244]), but no individual Website is so comprehensive that the P2 information-seeker only needs to look there. To do a thorough job, the P2 information-seeker needs to search many P2 sites, or risks missing valuable information. Although some of these sites are linked together, most are not. They need to be searched individually. Thoroughly searching ten sites is at least an afternoon's work. Hence, searching the "information superhighways" for particular information can be quite time-consuming. Even expert

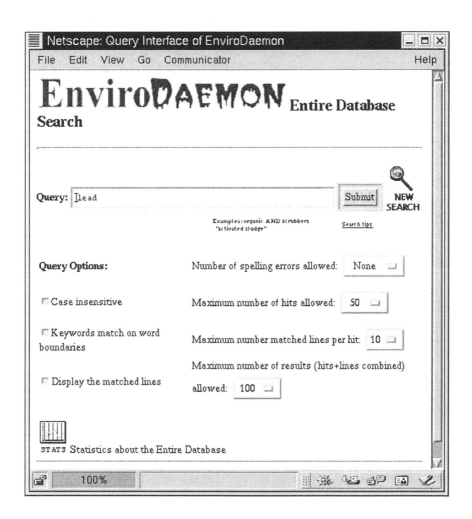

Figure 9.1.   Front-end interface for EnviroDaemon.

users who are familiar with environmental sites need to spend considerable time in searching, because new sources of data are appearing continually.

Generic search engines were designed to mine the Web. Given a search term, these engines return lists of Websites and specific references, often copiously. One could use one of the generic search engines to look up terms such as "pollution prevention" or a specific solvent and then wade through the resulting

Websites, hoping to chance upon helpful references. However, these search engines return so many "hits," most of which are unrelated to P2, that going through them all becomes burdensome.

2.1   AN INTELLIGENT LIBRARIAN

EnviroDaemon operates like the generic search engines, but its scope is focused on pollution prevention information. EnviroDaemon has expedited the gathering of P2 information by performing highly efficient, specific searches.

EnviroDaemon acts like an intelligent librarian, who in the vast library of the Internet, searches only specific collections devoted to pollution prevention. It keeps a catalog of items on more than 160 preselected P2 sites on the Internet. In response to a query, EnviroDaemon matches the search terms against its catalog. The user may further narrow the search by choosing one of six specialized search criteria:

- Pollution prevention and pollution control

- Regulatory

- International

- ISO 14000

- Recycling and materials exchange

- The entire P2 database

This service saves the information-seeker the time and trouble of searching dozens of Websites and, because the "hits" come only from P2 sites, it returns only that information that is most likely to be germane. To allow the user to select the most pertinent citations, EnviroDaemon returns the search item within the context of its surrounding text. Up to ten lines, as determined by the user, may be displayed.

The EnviroDaemon project followed the following steps, the first of which was to identify extant search engines, and to decide whether to tailor one for our efforts or to construct EnviroDaemon *de novo*. We decided to build a search engine de novo. The third step was to determine the appropriate Websites to mine for P2-related information. Next, EnviroDaemon was constructed and tested on the Web.

A look at the process by which EnviroDaemon finds, catalogs, and reports P2 information will give the reader an idea of its power and utility. It may also show the way to others who might wish to create similar custom search engines.

2.2   SELECTING TOOLS

Once the decision was made to build our search engine, a careful, detailed analysis was made to select the appropriate tools. We decided to use Harvest software tools [36], the Glimpse index/search mechanism [178] and the associated software that is required by Harvest and Glimpse (Glimpse stands for Global IMPlicit Search). Harvest employs a system of Gatherers and Brokers to retrieve and filter information. Glimpse indexes the information and provides a query system for rapidly searching through all of the gathered files.

Harvest software provides an integrated set of tools to gather, extract, organize, search, and replicate relevant information across the Internet. It possesses a flexible data-gathering architecture, which can be configured in various ways to create many types of indexes, making efficient use of Internet servers, network links, and index space on disk. Harvest permits users to build indexes using manually constructed templates (for maximum control over index content), automatically constructed templates (for easy coverage of large collections), or a combination of the two methods. Users also may extract structured (attribute-value pair) information from many different information formats and build indexes that permit these attributes to be referenced during queries (e.g., searching for all documents with a certain regular expression in the title field).

Measurements indicate that Harvest can reduce server load by a factor of over 6,000, network traffic by a factor of 60, and index space requirements by a factor of over 40 when building indexes compared with other Internet search engines, such as Archie, Wide Area Information Services (WAIS), and the World Wide Web Worm.

2.3   BUILDING ENVIRODAEMON

EnviroDaemon was originally designed and run on a Sun Sparc 5 computer with Solaris 2.3, with a 4GB SCSI drive. EnviroDaemon does not require a fast processor, but does require more memory. The critical factor affecting RAM usage is how much data EnviroDaemon tries to index. The more data, the more disk input-output is performed at query time, and the more RAM it takes to provide a reasonable disk buffer pool.

The amount of disk space required was decided after evaluating the size of the data to be indexed. Approximately 10 percents as much disk space as the total size of the data to be indexed is needed to hold the databases of **Gatherers** and **Brokers**. The actual space needs depend on the type of data indexed.

For example, PostScript achieves a much higher indexing space reduction than HTML because so much of the PostScript data (such as page positioning information) is discarded when building the index. An additional 50 MB of free disk space is required to run the Harvest Object Cache.

2.4   HARVEST SUBSYSTEM OVERVIEW

Harvest consists of a number of different subsystems. The **Gatherer** subsystem collects indexing information (such as keywords, author names, and titles) from the resources available at provider sites (such as FTP and Web servers). The **Broker** subsystem retrieves indexing information from one or more **Gatherers**, suppresses duplicate information, incrementally indexes the collected information, and provides a Web query interface to it. The **Replicator** subsystem efficiently replicates **Brokers** around the Internet. Information can be retrieved through the **Cache** subsystem. The Harvest Server Registry (HSR) is a distinguished **Broker** that holds information about each Harvest **Gatherer**, **Broker**, **Cache**, and **Replicator** in the Internet.

2.5   INSTALLING THE HARVEST SOFTWARE

Harvest **Gatherers** and **Brokers** can be configured in various ways. We have six different **Brokers** and **Gatherers** on our server. Each of the six search criteria has one dedicated **Broker** and **Gatherer** running. Since the **Gatherers** and **Brokers** are running locally, the search process is very efficient and quite fast.

In addition to the above platform requirements, we installed the following software packages:

- All Harvest servers require Perl v4.0 or higher (v5.0 is preferred).

- The Harvest **Broker** and **Gatherer** require GNU gzip v1.2.4 or higher.

- The Harvest **Broker** requires a Web server.

- Compiling Harvest requires GNU gcc v2.5.8 or higher.

- Compiling the Harvest **Broker** requires Flex v2.4.7 and Bison v1.22.

2.6   THE GATHERER

The **Gatherer** retrieves information resources using a variety of standard access methods (e.g., FTP, Gopher, HTTP, NNTP, and local files) and then summarizes those resources in various type-specific ways to generate structured indexing information. For example, a **Gatherer** can retrieve a technical report from an FTP archive, and then extract the author, title, and abstract from the paper to summarize the report. **Brokers** can then retrieve the indexing information from the **Gatherer**.

The **Gatherer** consists of a number of separate components. The **Gatherer** program reads a **Gatherer** configuration file and controls the overall process of enumerating and summarizing data objects. The structured indexing information that the **Gatherer** collects is represented as a list of attribute-value pairs using the Summary Object Interchange Format (SOIF). The gathered daemon serves the **Gatherer** database to **Brokers**. It remains in the background after a gathering session is complete. A stand-alone gathering program is a client for the gathered server. It can be used from the command line for testing and is used by a **Broker**. The **Gatherer** uses a local disk cache to store objects that it has retrieved.

Even though the gathered daemon remains in the background, the **Gatherer** does not automatically update or refresh its summary objects. Each object in the **Gatherer** has a time-to-live value: Objects remain in the database until they expire.

The **Gatherer** needs a list of the Uniform Resource Locators (URLs) from which it will gather indexing information, in our case the list of 160 pollution prevention servers. This list is specified in the **Gatherer** configuration file.

To prevent unwanted objects from being retrieved across the network, the **Gatherer** employs a series of filters. This dramatically reduces gathering time and network traffic. Since these filters are invoked at different times, they have different effects. The URL-filter, for example, allows only those Internet sites that have been pre-selected. After the **Gatherer** retrieves a document, it passes the document through a subsystem called **Essence**, which screens out certain documents from being indexed. **Essence** provides a powerful means of rejecting indexing that is based not only on file-naming conventions, but also on file contents (e.g., looking at strings at the beginning of a file or at UNIX "magic" numbers) and also on more sophisticated file-grouping schemes. Independent of these customizations, the **Gatherer** attempts to avoid retrieving objects when possible, by using a local disk cache of objects, and by using the HTTP "If-Modified-Since" request header.

Essence extracts indexing information from those documents that are not filtered out. **Essence** allows the **Gatherer** to collect indexing information from a wide variety of sources, using different techniques depending on the type of data. The **Essence** subsystem can determine the type of data (e.g., PostScript vs. HTML), "unravel" presentation nesting formats (such as compressed "tar" files), select which types of data to index (e.g., don't index Audio files), and then apply a type-specific extraction algorithm (called a summarizer) to the data to generate a content summary. Harvest is distributed with a stock set of type recognizers, presentation unnesters, candidate selectors, and summarizers that work well for many applications. We customized summarizers to change how they operate, and added summarizers for new types of data.

To reduce network traffic when restarting aborted gathering attempts, the **Gatherer** maintains a local disk cache of files that were retrieved successfully. By default, the **Gatherer**'s local disk cache is deleted after each successful completion. Since the remote server must be contacted whenever the **Gatherer** runs, we did not set up the **Gatherer** to run frequently. A typical value might be weekly or monthly, depending on how congested the network is and how important it is to have the most current data. By default, objects in the local disk cache expire after seven days.

2.7   THE BROKER

The **Broker** supports many different index/search engines. We used Harvest Broker Glimpse which has been used in many different search engines.

Particularly for large **Broker**s, it is often helpful to use more powerful queries because a simple search of a common term may take a long time. EnviroDaemon's query page contains several checkboxes that allow some control over query specification. Glimpse supports:

- Case-insensitive (lower and upper case letters are treated the same) and case sensitive queries;

- Matching parts of words, whole words, or phrases (like "resource recovery");

- Boolean (and/or) combinations of keywords;

- Approximate matches (e.g., allowing spelling errors); structured queries (allowing you to constrain matches to certain attributes);

- Displaying matched lines or entire matching records (e.g., for citations); specifying limits on the number of matches returned; and

- A limited form of regular expressions (e.g., allowing "wild card" expressions that match all words ending in a particular suffix).

EnviroDaemon allows the search to contain a number of errors. An error is either a deletion, insertion, or substitution of a single character. The Best Match option will find the match(es) with the least number of errors.

To allow popular Web browsers to mesh easily with EnviroDaemon, we implemented a Web interface to the **Broker**'s query manager and administrative interfaces. This interface consists of the following: HTML files that use Forms support to present a graphical user interface (GUI), Common Gateway Interface (CGI) programs that act as a gateway between the user and the **Broker**, and "help" files for the user. The **Broker** also needs to run in conjunction with a Web server.

Users go through the following steps when using the **Broker** to locate information:

1. The user issues a query to the **Broker**.

2. The **Broker** processes the query, and returns the query results to the user.

3. The user can then view content summaries from the result set, or access the URLs from the result set directly.

The **Broker** retrieves indexing information from **Gatherers** or other **Brokers** through its **Collector** interface. A list of collection points is specified along with the host of the remote **Gatherer** or **Broker**, and the query filter if there is one. The **Broker** supports various types of collections. EnviroDaemon **Brokers** use indexing information retrieved from **Gatherers** through incremental collections.

2.8   GLIMPSE

Glimpse is an indexing and query system that searches through files very quickly. Glimpse supports most of `agrep`'s options which is a more powerful version of `grep` and includes approximate matching (e.g., finding misspelled words), Boolean queries, and even some limited forms of regular expressions. For example, if one is looking for a word such as "needle" anywhere in the file system, all that one needs to specify is, "glimpse needle," and all the lines containing the word "needle" will appear preceded by the file name. To use Glimpse, we first index our files with Glimpseindex, which is typically run every night.

The speed of Glimpse depends mainly on the number and sizes of the files that contain a match, and only secondarily on the total size of all indexed files. If the pattern is reasonably uncommon, then all matches will be reported in a few seconds, even if the indexed files total 500 MB or more.

Glimpse includes an optional new compression program, called **Case**, which permits Glimpse (and `agrep`) to search compressed files without having to decompress them. The search is significantly faster when the files are compressed.

Glimpse can search for Boolean combinations of "attribute-value" terms by using the EnviroDaemon's SOIF parser library. To search this way, the index is made by using the -s option of Glimpseindex (this is used in conjunction with other Glimpseindex options). For Glimpse and Glimpseindex to recognize "structured" files, they must be in SOIF format. Any string can serve as an attribute name. The scope of Boolean operations changes from records (lines) to whole files when structured queries are used in Glimpse.

Glimpse's index is word based. A pattern that contains more than one word cannot be found in the index. The way Glimpse overcomes this weakness is by splitting any multi-word pattern into its set of words, and looking for files in the index that contain the whole set.

3.   ED WITH HIERARCHICAL SEARCH

This section describes some precise search approaches in the environmental domain that locate information according to syntactic criteria, augmented by the utilization of information in a certain context. The main emphasis lies in the treatment of structured knowledge, where essential aspects about the topic of interest are encoded not only by the individual items, but also by their relationships among each other. Examples for such structured knowledge are hypertext documents, diagrams, logical and chemical formulae. Benefits of this approach are enhanced precision and approximate search in EnviroDaemon.

We recently combine EnviroDaemon with a Hierarchical Information Search Tool (HIST), which permits queries based on hierarchical structure. The rationale for this extension is that search conditions incorporating both keyword and structure-based queries will help the user more precisely locate information. Figure 9.2 shows the front-end interface for EnviroDaemon with HIST. The query in the figure is to search for documents with the word "energy" in an h1 tag.

Many search engines have their distinctive features: single domain, multi-domain, meta-search engines which are front-ends of other search engines. However, few of them make attempts to exploit the explicit underlying hypertext tags in a single domain. Our search filtering tool, HIST, however, is able to exploit the full syntactic detail of any hypertext markup language and provide hierarchical query capability.

The essence of HIST is to permit end users to specify in which parts of a document a keyword should appear: in a document title, in a section header, somewhere in a paragraph, or in a table. This allows more precise control over the search process, and hence, results in much better selection of relevant material. Another salient feature of HIST is the idea of "fuzzy search." The documents returned by HIST do not have to be exact matches. Users have control over how similar the target document should be in the hierarchical query. Furthermore, at the speed that the Web technology standard is proceeding, an information retrieval tool must be able to meet the challenges of the next generation of the document standard on the Web. Since HIST is based on the Document Type Definition (DTD) Model, it is suitable for the new emerging document exchange standard for the Web, namely Extensible Markup Language (XML).

HIST does not replace the existing EnviroDaemon search engine. It enhances the EnviroDaemon for information searching on associated environment-related topics. For a general search on the Web, where the user has little knowledge about the nature of the document (in terms of document structure), we still encourage the use of EnviroDaemon. On the other hand, when the situation

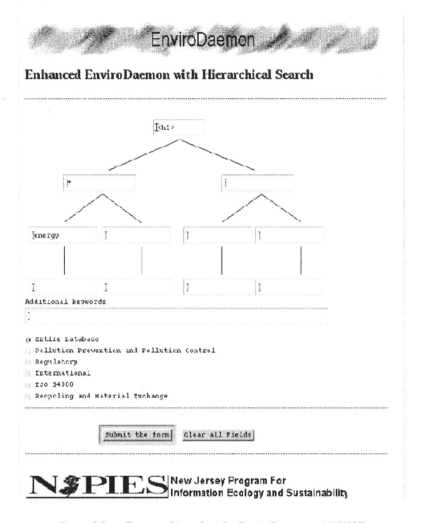

Figure 9.2.　　Front-end interface for EnviroDaemon with HIST.

permits, the HIST tool will be extremely useful when the target document structure is partially or completely known.

HIST is composed of the following modules: Query Processor, SGML/XML Parser, HTML Parser, Tree Comparator, Retrieval Agents, and Front-end Interface. Figure 9.3 illustrates the HIST architecture.

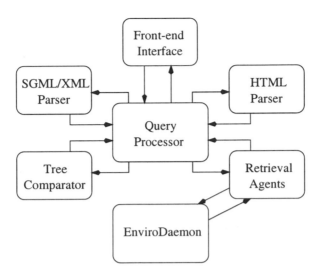

Figure 9.3.   HIST system architecture.

The Query Processor handles queries from the Front-end Interface and invokes the Tree Comparator when necessary. The Retrieval Agents retrieve the actual HTML pages that satisfy keywords specified in the Front-end Interface from EnviroDaemon. The HTML Parser translates the HTML pages into hierarchical tree structures based on the HTML DTD. The SGML/XML Parser translates the HTML pages into hierarchical tree structures based on a document's DTD. The Tree Comparator contains various approximate tree and string matching programs.

As many previous approaches have suggested, to analyze documents from the Web, the first step is to derive a scheme that describes the HTML page. While a specially designed schema provides a structural way of analyzing a hypertext document, much of the semantics associated with the document is lost after the transformation process. Our approach differs from others in that we do not design a special schema, but, instead work with the DTD associated with hypertext documents.

With DTD in hand, we can parse each hypertext document using its own DTD, capitalizing on the fact that the DTD provides not only the grammatical information, but also semantic information. For HTML documents, we can parse them using HTML DTD 4.0. For the article type of SGML/XML docu-

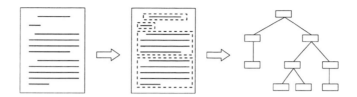

Figure 9.4.   Converting a hypertext document to a labeled tree using DTD.

ments, we can parse it with article DTD. The parsed tree structure of a typical document is illustrated in Figure 9.4. In this figure, the logical structure of the document is identified by the parser, which is denoted by dashed rectangles.

4.   A HIERARCHICAL QUERY LANGUAGE

EnviroDaemon with HIST has a query language that is similar to WAQL described in Chapter 2. Consider the hierarchical query in Figure 9.5(a). This query is to find the HTML pages containing the word "database" in an H1 header followed by a paragraph consisting of "object" followed by "relational." The * notation in the internal node of the query is a "variable length don't care" (VLDC) symbol, which represents an unspecified portion of a document as described below. The query may be issued when an individual intends to locate some HTML pages available on the Internet while conducting database-related research. Here the user places an emphasis on "database" and is interested in only those HTML pages having the word in an H1 header, rather than in any other place of a document.

To process such a hierarchical query using EnviroDaemon with HIST, we take the conjunction of the keywords appearing in the query and invoke our EnviroDaemon search engine to find the HTML pages containing these keywords. The EnviroDaemon search engine returns a collection of candidate uniform resource locators (URLs), ranked based on their relevance to the keywords. Duplicate URLs are deleted and a document corresponding to each matching URL is then retrieved using a libwww-Perl4 module, with time-outs set to 20 seconds to account for a busy network or failed connections. Each retrieved HTML document is then transformed into a hierarchical tree structure based on the DTD described earlier. The transformed tree structures then become candidate HTML trees to be compared with hierarchical query trees. Figure 9.5(b)

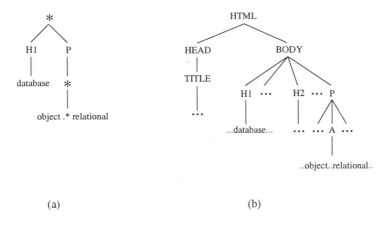

     (a)   (b)

Figure 9.5.   (a) An hierarchical search pattern; (b) an HTML tree.

shows an example tree for an HTML page. The tree is rooted, labeled and ordered (i.e., each node has a label and the order of siblings is important). An internal node represents an HTML tag and a leaf contains the associated text.

Our system compares the query tree with each candidate HTML tree using a previously developed approximate tree matching algorithm [284] in conjunction with regular expression matching on leaves when required. The URLs of qualified pages are then returned. In comparing the query tree with an HTML tree, a VLDC can be matched, at no cost, with a path or portion of a path in the HTML tree. The tree matching algorithm calculates the minimum edit distance between the query tree and the HTML tree after implicitly computing an optimal substitution for the VLDCs in the query tree, allowing zero or more cuttings at nodes from the HTML tree [284]. Cutting at a node n means removing the subtree rooted at n.

Given two trees T_1 and T_2, the algorithm runs in time $O(|T_1| \times |T_2| \times \min\{depth(T_1), leaves(T_1)\} \times \min\{depth(T_2), leaves(T_2)\})$. Thus, for example, in matching the query tree in Figure 9.5(a) and the HTML tree in Figure 9.5(b), the $*$ at the root in Figure 9.5(a) would be matched with (or instantiated into) the nodes HTML and BODY in Figure 9.5(b), and the $*$ underneath P in Figure 9.5(a) would be matched with the node A (i.e., the Anchor tag) in Figure 9.5(b). The nodes H1, "database" and "object.*relational" in Figure 9.5(a) would be matched with their corresponding nodes in Figure 9.5(b). All the other nodes in Figure 9.5(b) are cut.

5.   SUMMARY

EnviroDaemon has proven to be useful by rapidly returning results that are focused on pollution prevention (P2) and other environmental topics such as ISO 14000. By limiting its scope to P2-related Websites, EnviroDaemon can afford to be more thorough, searching whole documents rather than just titles and keywords. The resulting "hits" are embedded in up to ten lines of surrounding text; knowing the context of how the term was employed allows the user to thin out inappropriate sites without taking the time to actually visit them. EnviroDaemon obviates the need to look through one Website after another, or to know beforehand which sites are most promising.

In this chapter, we also described the EnviroDaemon with a Hierarchical Information Search Tool (HIST) on the Web. The system makes several contributions. It is context-specific and one of two environmentally directed search engines on the Web (the other being the proprietary EnviroSources [86]). It permits more detailed search than existing search engines. Additionally, it allows several kinds of approximate search at different levels:

- approximate search on the structural level, based on edit distance between structures;

- approximate search on the string level;

- variable length don't cares on the structural level; and

- any combination of the above.

It provides a query language that allows users to flexibly combine a variety of constructs and has proven to be useful for the Web environment where the languages employed are HTML, SGML, and XML. EnviroDaemon with HIST promises to save users from drowning in an information sea and is generic enough to be useful for the Web and intranets.

References

[1] S. Abiteboul, P. Buneman, and D. Suciu. *Data on the Web: From Relations to Semistructured Data and XML*. Morgan Kaufmann, San Francisco, California, 2000.

[2] S. Abiteboul, D. Quass, J. McHugh, J. Widom, and J. L. Wiener. The Lore query language for semistructured data. *International Journal on Digital Libraries*, 1(1):68–88, 1997.

[3] S. Abiteboul and V. Vianu. Queries and computation on the Web. In *Proceedings of International Conference on Database Theory*, pages 262–275, Delphi, Greece, January 1997.

[4] R. Agrawal, J. Gehrke, D. Gunopulos, and P. Raghavan. Automatic subspace clustering of high dimensional data for data mining applications. In *Proceedings of the 1998 ACM SIGMOD International Conference on Management of Data*, pages 94–105, Seattle, Washington, June 1998.

[5] R. Agrawal, T. Imielinski, and A. Swami. Mining association rules between sets of items in large databases. In *Proceedings of the 1993 ACM SIGMOD International Conference on Management of Data*, pages 207–216, Washington, D.C., May 1993.

[6] R. Agrawal, H. Mannila, R. Srikant, H. Toivonen, and A. I. Verkamo. Fast discovery of association rules. In U. M. Fayyad, G. Piatetsky-Shapiro, P. Smyth, and R. Uthurusamy, editors, *Advances in Knowledge Discovery and Data Mining*, pages 307–328, Cambridge, Massachusetts, 1996. MIT Press.

[7] R. Agrawal and R. Srikant. Fast algorithms for mining association rules. In *Proceedings of the 20th International Conference on Very Large Data Bases*, pages 487–499, Santiago, Chile, September 1994.

[8] R. Agrawal and R. Srikant. Mining sequential patterns. In *Proceedings of the 11th International Conference on Data Engineering*, pages 3–14, Zurich, Switzerland, September 1995.

[9] A. Agresti. *An Introduction to Categorical Data Analysis*. John Wiley & Sons, New York, New York, 1996.

[10] A. V. Aho, J. E. Hopcroft, and J. D. Ullman. *The Design and Analysis of Computer Algorithms*. Addison–Wesley, New York, New York, 1994.

[11] J. Allan, J. Carbonell, G. Doddington, J. Yamron, and Y. Yang. Topic detection and tracking pilot study. In *Proceedings of the DARPA Broadcast News Transcription and Understanding Workshop*, pages 194–218, San Francisco, California, February 1998.

[12] J. Allan, R. Papka, and V. Lavrenko. On-line news event detection and tracking. In *Proceedings of the 21st Annual International ACM SIGIR Conference on Research and Development in Information Retrieval*, pages 37–45, Melbourne, Australia, August 1998.

[13] AltaVista. http://altavista.digital.com.

[14] A. Amir, M. Lewenstein, and N. Lewenstein. Pattern matching in hypertext. In *Proceedings of the Workshop on Algorithms and Data Structures*, pages 160–173, Halifax, Nova Scotia, Canada, August 1997.

[15] AMORE. http://www.ccrl.com/amore.

[16] M. Ankerst, M. Breunig, H.-P. Kriegel, and J. Sander. OPTICS: Ordering points to identify the clustering structure. In *Proceedings of the 1999 ACM SIGMOD International Conference on Management of Data*, pages 49–60, Philadelphia, Pennsylvania, June 1999.

[17] Apache Web Server. http://www.apache.org.

[18] M. Aragújo, G. Navarro, and N. Ziviani. Large text searching allowing errors. In *Proceedings of the South American Workshop on String Processing*, pages 2–20, Valparaíso, Chile, 1997.

[19] AskJeeves. http://www.askjeeves.com.

[20] P. Atzeni and G. Mecca. Cut and paste. In *Proceedings of the 16th ACM SIGACT-SIGMOD-SIGART Symposium on Principles of Database Systems*, Tucson, Arizona, May 1997.

[21] P. Atzeni, G. Mecca, and P. Merialdo. To weave the Web. In *Proceedings of the 23rd International Conference on Very Large Data Bases*, Athens, Greece, August 1997.

[22] J. R. Bach, C. Fuller, A. Gupta, A. Hampapur, B. Horwitz, R. Jain, and C. Shu. Virage image search engine: An open framework for image management. In *Proceedings of the SPIE Conference on Storage and Retrieval for Image and Video Databases*, pages 76–87, San Jose, California, February 1996.

[23] R. Baeza-Yates and B. Ribeiro-Neto. *Modern Information Retrieval*. ACM Press, Addison–Wesley, New York, New York, 1999.

[24] R. Bayer and E. M. McCreight. Organization and maintenance of large ordered indexes. *Acta Informatica*, 1(3):173–189, 1972.

[25] R. Bayer and K. Unterauer. Prefix B-trees. *ACM Transactions on Database Systems*, 2(1):11–26, 1977.

[26] N. J. Belkin and W. B. Croft. Information filtering and information retrieval: Two sides of the same coin? *Communications of the ACM*, 35(12):29–38, 1992.

[27] B. Berendt and M. Spiliopoulou. Analyzing navigation behavior in Web sites integrating multiple information systems. *VLDB Journal: Special Issue on Databases and the Web*, 9(1):56–75, 2000.

[28] T. Berners-Lee, R. Cailliau, A. Luotonen, H. F. Nielsen, and A. Secret. The World Wide Web. *Communications of the ACM*, 37(8):76–82, 1994.

[29] M. J. A. Berry and G. Linoff. *Mastering Data Mining: The Art and Science of Customer Relationship Management*. John Wiley & Sons, New York, New York, 1999.

[30] A. Berson, S. Smith, and K. Thearling. *Building Data Mining Applications for CRM*. McGraw-Hill, New York, New York, 1999.

[31] A. Berson and S. J. Smith. *Data Warehousing, Data Mining, and OLAP*. McGraw-Hill, New York, New York, 1997.

[32] J. C. Bezdek and S. K. Pal. *Fuzzy Models for Pattern Recognition: Methods That Search for Structures in Data*. IEEE Press, 1992.

[33] K. Bharat, A. Broder, M. Henzinger, P. Kumar, and S. Venkatasubramian. The connectivity server: Fast access to linkage information on the Web. In

Proceedings of the 7th International World Wide Web Conference, pages 469–477, Brisbane, Australia, April 1998.

[34] K. Bharat and M. R. Henzinger. Improved algorithms for topic distillation in a hyperlinked environment. In *Proceedings of the 21st Annual International ACM SIGIR Conference on Research and Development in Information Retrieval*, pages 104–111, Melbourne, Australia, August 1998.

[35] BioCrawler. http://www.biocrawler.com.

[36] C. M. Bowman, P. B. Danzig, D. R. Hardy, U. Manber, and M. F. Schwartz. The Harvest information discovery and access system. In *Proceedings of the 2nd International World Wide Web Conference*, Chicago, Illinois, October 1994.

[37] R. S. Boyer and J. S. Moore. A fast string searching algorithm. *Communications of the ACM*, 20(10):762–772, 1977.

[38] D. Briandais. File searching using variable length keys. In *Proceedings of the AFIPS Western JCC*, pages 295–298, San Francisco, California, 1959.

[39] E. Brill. A simple rule–based part–of–speech tagger. In *Proceedings of the 3rd Conference on Applied Natural Language Processing*, Trento, Italy, April 1992.

[40] S. Brin and L. Page. The anatomy of a large-scale hypertextual Web search engine. In *Proceedings of the 7th International World Wide Web Conference*, pages 107–117, Brisbane, Australia, April 1998.

[41] A. G. Büchner, M. Baumgarten, S. Anand, and M. Mulvenna. Navigation pattern discovery from Internet data. In *Proceedings of the Web Knowledge and Data Discovery Conference*, San Diego, California, August 1999.

[42] A. G. Büchner and M. D. Mulvenna. Discovering Internet marketing intelligence through online analytical Web usage mining. *ACM SIGMOD Record*, 27(4):54–61, 1999.

[43] P. Buneman. Semistructured data. In *Proceedings of the 16th ACM SIGACT-SIGMOD-SIGART Symposium on Principles of Database Systems*, pages 117–121, Tucson, Arizona, May 1997.

[44] P. Buneman, S. Davidson, G. Hillebrand, and D. Suciu. A query language and optimization techniques for unstructured data. In *Proceedings of the*

1996 ACM SIGMOD International Conference on Management of Data, pages 505–516, Montreal, Canada, June 1996.

[45] P. Buneman, S. B. Davidson, and D. Suciu. Programming constructs for unstructured data. In *Proceedings of the 5th International Workshop on Database Programming Languages*, page 12, Umbria, Italy, September 1995.

[46] M. Burner. Crawling towards eternity: Building an archive of the World Wide Web. *Web Techniques Magazine*, 2(5), 1997.

[47] Y. Cai, N. Cercone, and J. Han. Attribute-oriented induction in relational databases. In G. Piatetsky-Shapiro and W. J. Frawley, editors, *Knowledge Discovery in Databases*, pages 213–228, Cambridge, Massachusetts, 1991. AAAI/MIT Press.

[48] J. Callan. Searching for needles in a world of haystacks. *IEEE Data Engineering Bulletin*, 23(3):33–37, 2000.

[49] R. G. Cattell and D. K. Barry, editors. *The Object Database Standard: ODMG 2.0*. Morgan Kaufmann, San Francisco, California, 1997.

[50] S. Chakrabarti, B. Dom, D. Gibson, J. Kleinberg, S. Kumar, P. Raghavan, S. Rajagopalan, and A. Tomkins. Mining the link structure of the World Wide Web. *IEEE Computer*, 32(8):60–67, 1999.

[51] S. Chakrabarti, B. Dom, D. Gibson, S. R. Kumar, P. Raghavan, and S. Rajagopalan. Experiments in topic distillation. In *Proceedings of the ACM SIGIR Workshop on Hypertext Information Retrieval on the Web*, Melbourne, Australia, 1998.

[52] S. Chakrabarti, B. Dom, P. Raghavan, S. Rajagopalanand, D. Gibson, and J. M. Kleinberg. Automatic resource compilation by analyzing hyperlink structure and associated text. In *Proceedings of the 7th International World Wide Web Conference*, pages 65–74, Brisbane, Australia, April 1998.

[53] S. Chakrabarti, M. van den Berg, and B. Dom. Focused crawling: A new approach to topic-specific Web resource discovery. In *Proceedings of the 8th International World Wide Web Conference*, pages 1623–1640, Toronto, Canada, May 1999.

[54] R. Chandrasekar and B. Srinivas. Gleaning information from the Web: Using syntax to filter out irrelevant information. In *Proceedings of the AAAI*

Spring Symposium on Natural Language Processing form the WWW, Stanford, California, March 1997.

[55] S. Chang, J. Smith, M. Beigi, and A. Benitez. Visual information retrieval from large distributed online repositories. *Communications of the ACM*, 40(12):63–71, 1997.

[56] S. Chawathe, H. Garcia-Molina, J. Hammer, K. Ireland, Y. Papakonstanti-nou, J. Ullman, and J. Widom. The TSIMMIS project: Integration of het-erogeneous information sources. In *Proceedings of the IPSJ Conference*, pages 7–18, Tokyo, Japan, October 1994.

[57] J. Chen, D. J. DeWitt, F. Tian, and Y. Wang. NiagaraCQ: A scalable continuous query system for Internet databases. In *Proceedings of the 2000 ACM SIGMOD International Conference on Management of Data*, pages 379–390, Dallas, Texas, May 2000.

[58] M. Chen, J. Park, and P. Yu. Data mining for path traversal patterns in a Web environment. In *Proceedings of the 16th International Conference on Distributed Computing Systems*, pages 385–392, Hong Kong, May 1996.

[59] J. Cho, H. Garcia-Molina, and L. Page. Efficient crawling through URL ordering. In *Proceedings of the 7th International World Wide Web Con-ference*, pages 161–172, Brisbane, Australia, April 1998.

[60] V. Christophides, S. Cluet, and G. Moerkotte. Evaluating queries with generalized path expressions. In *Proceedings of the 1996 ACM SIGMOD International Conference on Management of Data*, pages 413–422, Mon-treal, Canada, June 1996.

[61] K. Cios, W. Pedrycz, and R. Swiniarski. *Data Mining Methods for Knowl-edge Discovery*. Kluwer Academic Publishers, Norwell, Massachusetts, 1998.

[62] W. Cleveland. *Visualizing Data*. Hobart Press, Summit, New Jersey, 1993.

[63] Clever Project. http://www.almaden.ibm.com/cs/k53/clever.html.

[64] E. F. Codd, S. B. Codd, and C. T. Salley. Beyond decision support. *Computer World*, 27, May 1993.

[65] W. Cohen, A. McCallum, and D. Quass. Learning to understand the Web. *IEEE Data Engineering Bulletin*, 23(3):17–24, 2000.

[66] R. Cooley, B. Mobasher, and J. Srivastava. Web mining: Information and pattern discovery on the World Wide Web. In *Proceedings of the 9th IEEE International Conference on Tools with Artificial Intelligence*, pages 558–567, 1997.

[67] R. Cooley, B. Mobasher, and J. Srivastava. Data preparation for mining World Wide Web browsing patterns. *Knowledge and Information Systems*, 1(1):5–32, 1999.

[68] Cora. http://www.cora.justresearch.com.

[69] M. Craven, D. DiPasquo, D. Freitag, A. McCallum, T. M. Mitchell, K. Nigam, and S. Slattery. Learning to extract symbolic knowledge from the World Wide Web. In *Proceedings of the 15th National Conference on Artificial Intelligence (AAAI-98)*, 1998.

[70] W. B. Croft. What do people want from information retrieval? *D-Lib Magazine*, November, 1995.

[71] W. B. Croft, editor. *Advances in Information Retrieval: Recent Research from the Center for Intelligent Information Retrieval*. Kluwer Academic Publishers, Norwell, Massachusetts, 2000.

[72] D. R. Cutting. A practical part–of–speech tagger. In *Proceedings of the 3rd Conference on Applied Natural Language Processing*, Trento, Italy, April 1992.

[73] D. R. Cutting, D. R. Karger, and J. O. Pedersen. Scatter/Gather: A cluster-based approach to browsing large document collections. In *Proceedings of the 15th Annual International ACM SIGIR Conference on Research and Development in Information Retrieval*, pages 318–329, Copenhagen, Denmark, June 1992.

[74] B. Daille. Study and implementation of combined techniques for automatic extraction of terminology. In *Proceedings of the 32nd Annual Meeting of the Association for Computational Linguistics*, Las Cruces, New Maxico, July 1994.

[75] Deja News. http://www.deja.com.

[76] A. Deutsch, M. Fernandez, D. Florescu, A. Levy, and D. Suciu. XML-QL: A query language for XML. Technical report, World Wide Web Consortium, 1998. http://www.w3.org/TR/NOTE-xml-ql/.

[77] J. L. Devore. *Probability and Statistics for Engineering and the Sciences*. Duxbury Press, New York, New York, 1995.

[78] M. Diligenti, F. Coetzee, S. Lawrence, C. L. Giles, and M. Gori. Focused crawling using context graphs. In *Proceedings of the 26th International Conference on Very Large Data Bases*, Cairo, Egypt, September 2000.

[79] Direct Hit. http://www.directhit.com.

[80] Ditto. http://www.ditto.com.

[81] D. Dreilinger and A. E. Howe. Experiences with selecting search engines using metasearch. *ACM Transactions on Information Systems*, 15(3):195–222, July 1997.

[82] R. Duda and P. Hart. *Pattern Classifications and Scene Analysis*. John Wiley & Sons, New York, New York, 1973.

[83] S. T. Dumais, J. Platt, D. Hecherman, and M. Sahami. Inductive learning algorithms and representations for text categorization. In *Proceedings of ACM CIKM International Conference on Information and Knowledge Management*, Bethesda, Maryland, 1998.

[84] D. Eichmann. The RBSE spider - Balancing effective search against Web load. In *Proceedings of the 1st International World Wide Web Conference*, pages 113–120, 1994.

[85] ElectricMonk. http://www.electricmonk.com.

[86] EnviroSources. http://www.envirosources.com.

[87] M. Ester, H.-P. Kriegel, J. Sander, and X. Xu. A density-based algorithm for discovering clusters in large spatial databases. In *Proceedings of the 2nd International Conference on Knowledge Discovery and Data Mining*, pages 226–231, Portland, Oregon, August 1996.

[88] Excalibur. http://www.excalib.com.

[89] Excite. http://www.excite.com.

[90] C. Faloutsos and S. Christodoulakis. Signature files: An access method for documents and its analytical performance evaluation. *ACM Transactions on Office Information Systems*, 2(4):267–288, 1984.

[91] C. Faloutsos and S. Christodoulakis. Description and performance analysis of signature file methods. *ACM Transactions on Information Systems*, 5(3):237–257, 1987.

[92] C. Faloutsos, M. Flocker, W. Niblack, D. Petkovic, W. Equitz, and R. Barver. Efficient and effective querying by image content. Technical report, IBM, 1993.

[93] FAST Search. http://www.alltheweb.com.

[94] U. Fayyad and R. Uthurusamy. Data mining and knowledge discovery in databases. *Communications of the ACM*, 39(11):24–26, 1996.

[95] U. M. Fayyad, G. Piatetsky-Shapiro, P. Smyth, and R. Uthurusamy, editors. *Advances in Knowledge Discovery and Data Mining*. AAAI/MIT Press, Cambridge, Massachusetts, 1996.

[96] R. Feldman, I. Dagan, and W. Kloegsen. Efficient algorithms for mining and manipulating associations in texts. In *Proceedings of the 13th European Meeting on Cybernetics and Research*, 1996.

[97] R. Feldman, M. Fresko, Y. Kinar, Y. Lindell, O. Liphstat, M. Rajman, Y. Schler, and O. Zamir. Text mining at the term level. In *Proceedings of the 2nd European Symposium on Principles of Data Mining and Knowledge Discovery*, pages 65–73, Nantes, France, September 1998.

[98] R. Feldman and H. Hirsh. Mining associations in text in presence of background knowledge. In *Proceedings of the 2nd International Conference on Knowledge Discovery and Data Mining*, pages 343–346, Portland, Oregon, 1996.

[99] M. Fernandez and J. Robie. XML Query Data Model. Technical report, World Wide Web Consortium, 2000. http://www.w3.org/TR/query-datamodel/.

[100] J. Fiscus, G. Doddington, J. Garofolo, and A. Martin. NIST's 1998 topic detection and tracking evaluation (PTDT2). In *Proceedings of the DARPA Broadcast News Transcription and Understanding Workshop*, pages 19–26, Herndon, Virginia, February 1999.

[101] G. W. Flake, S. Lawrence, and C. L. Giles. Efficient identification of Web communities. In *Proceedings of the 6th ACM SIGKDD International Conference on Knowledge Discovery and Data Mining*, pages 150–160, Boston, Massachusetts, August 2000.

[102] M. Flickner, H. Sawhney, W. Niblack, J. Ashley, Q. Huang, B. Dom, M. Gorkani, J. Hafner, D. Lee, D. Petkovic, D. Steele, and P. Yonker. Query by image and video content: The QBIC system. *IEEE Computer*, 28(9):23–32, 1995.

[103] J. Fürnkranz, T. M. Mitchell, and E. Riloff. A case study in using linguistic phrases for text categorization on the WWW. In *Working Notes*

of the 1998 AAAI/ICML Workshop on Learning for Text Categorization, 1998.

[104] H. Garcia-Molina, J. Widom, and J. D. Ullman. *Database System Implementation*. Prentice Hall, Upper Saddle River, New Jersey, 2000.

[105] M. N. Garofalakis, R. Rastogi, S. Seshadri, and K. Shim. Data mining and the Web: Past, present and future. In *Proceedings of the WIDM99 Conference*, pages 43–47, Kansas City, Missouri, 1999.

[106] D. Gibson, J. M. Kleinberg, and P. Raghavan. Inferring Web communities from link topology. In *Proceedings of the 9th ACM Conference on Hypertext and Hypermedia*, pages 225–234, Pittsburgh, Pennsylvania, June 1998.

[107] A. Glossbrenner and E. Glossbrenner. *Search Engines for the World Wide Web*. Peachpit Press, Berkeley, California, 1998.

[108] E. J. Glover, S. Lawrence, W. P. Birmingham, and C. L. Giles. Architecture of a metasearch engine that supports user information needs. In *Proceedings of the ACM CIKM International Conference on Information and Knowledge Management*, Kansas City, Missouri, 1999.

[109] Go (Infoseek). http://www.go.com.

[110] D. Goldberg. *Genetic Algorithms in Search, Optimization, and Machine Learning*. Addison–Wesley, Reading, Massachusetts, 1989.

[111] C. Goldfarb. *The XML Handbook*. Prentice Hall, Upper Saddle River, New Jersey, 1999.

[112] R. Goldman and J. Widom. WSQ/DSQ: A practical approach for combined querying of databases and the Web. In *Proceedings of the 2000 ACM SIGMOD International Conference on Management of Data*, pages 285–296, Dallas, Texas, May 2000.

[113] G. H. Gonnet. Examples of PAT applied to the Oxford English Dictionary. Technical report, University of Waterloo, 1987.

[114] Google. http://www.google.com.

[115] G. Grahne, L. Lakshmanan, and X. Wang. Efficient mining of constrained correlated sets. In *Proceedings of the 16th International Conference on Data Engineering*, pages 512–521, San Diego, California, February 2000.

[116] S. Guha, R. Rastogi, and K. Shim. Cure: An efficient clustering algorithm for large databases. In *Proceedings of the 1998 ACM SIGMOD*

International Conference on Management of Data, pages 73–84, Seattle, Washington, June 1998.

[117] S. Guha, R. Rastogi, and K. Shim. Rock: A robust clustering algorithm for categorical attributes. In *Proceedings of the 15th International Conference on Data Engineering*, pages 512–521, Sydney, Australia, March 1999.

[118] J. Han and Y. Fu. Discovery of multiple-level association rules from large databases. In *Proceedings of the 21st International Conference on Very Large Data Bases*, pages 420–431, Zurich, Switzerland, September 1995.

[119] J. Han, Y. Fu, W. Wang, J. Chiang, W. Gong, K. Koperski, D. Li, Y. Lu, A. Rajan, N. Stefanovic, B. Xia, and O. R. Zaiane. DBMiner: A system for mining knowledge in large relational databases. In *Proceedings of the 2nd International Conference on Knowledge Discovery and Data Mining*, pages 250–255, Portland, Oregon, August 1996.

[120] J. Han and M. Kamber. *Data Mining: Concepts and Techniques*. Morgan Kaufmann, San Francisco, California, 2000.

[121] J. Han, S. Nishio, H. Kawano, and W. Wang. Generalization-based data mining in object-oriented databases using an object-cube model. *Data and Knowledge Engineering*, 25:55–97, 1998.

[122] V. Harmandas, M. Sanderson, and M. Dunlop. Image retrieval by hypertext links. In *Proceedings of the 20th Annual International ACM SIGIR Conference on Research and Development in Information Retrieval*, pages 296–303, Philadelphia, Pennsylvania, July 1997.

[123] J. A. Hartigan. *Clustering Algorithms*. John Wiley & Sons, New York, New York, 1975.

[124] M. J. Healey, J. T. Lewis, and G. Samtani. Using EnviroDaemon to search the Internet for environmental information and building custom search engines. *Environmental Quality Management*, 8(1):103–109, 1998.

[125] M. J. Healey, J. T. L. Wang, G. Chang, A. Revankar, and G. Samtani. Precise environmental searches: EnviroDaemon with hierarchical information search. *Environmental Quality Management*, 9(1):51–62, 1999.

[126] M. A. Hearst. Untangling text data mining. In *Proceedings of the 37th Annual Meeting of the Association for Computational Linguistics*, College Park, Maryland, August 1999.

[127] D. Heckerman. Bayesian networks for knowledge discovery. In U. M. Fayyad, G. Piatetsky-Shapiro, P. Smyth, and R. Uthurusamy, editors, *Advances in Knowledge Discovery and Data Mining*, pages 273–305, Cambridge, Massachusetts, 1996. MIT Press.

[128] J. Hertz, A. Krogh, and R. G. Palmer. *Introduction to the Theory of Neural Computation*. Addison–Wesley, Reading, Massachusetts, 1991.

[129] A. Heydon and M. Najork. Mercator: A scalable, extensible Web crawler. *World Wide Web*, 2(4):219–229, 1999.

[130] A. Hinneburg and D. A. Keim. An efficient approach to clustering in large multimedia databases with noise. In *Proceedings of the 4th International Conference on Knowledge Discovery and Data Mining*, pages 58–65, New York, New York, August 1998.

[131] Hit List by Accrue Software. http://www.accrue.com.

[132] J. E. Hopcroft and J. D. Ullman. *Introduction to Automata Theory, Language and Computation*. Addison-Wesley, New York, New York, 1979.

[133] HotBot. http://www.hotbot.com.

[134] Z. Huang. Extensions to the k-means algorithm for clustering large data sets. *Data Mining and Knowledge Discovery*, 2:283–304, 1998.

[135] T. Imielinski and A. Virmani. MSQL: A query language for database mining. *Data Mining and Knowledge Discovery*, 3(4):373–408, 1999.

[136] Inktomi. http://www.inktomi.com.

[137] Inktomi/NEC press release. Web surpasses one billion documents, January 2000. http://www.inktomi.com.

[138] W. H. Inmon. *Building the Data Warehouse*. John Wiley & Sons, New York, New York, 1996.

[139] A. K. Jain and R. C. Dubes. *Algorithms for Clustering Data*. Prentice Hall, Englewood Cliffs, New Jersey, 1988.

[140] M. James. *Classification Algorithms*. John Wiley & Sons, New York, New York, 1985.

[141] R. A. Johnson and D. A. Wichern. *Applied Multivariate Statistical Analysis*. Prentice Hall, Upper Saddle River, New Jersey, 1992.

[142] K. P. Joshi, A. Joshi, Y. Yesha, and R. Krishnapuram. Warehousing and mining Web logs. In *Proceedings of the 2nd ACM CIKM Workshop on Web Information and Data Management*, pages 63–68, Kansas City, Missouri, 1999.

[143] M. Kamber, J. Han, and J. Y. Chiang. Metarule-guided mining of multidimensional association rules using data cubes. In *Proceedings of the 3rd International Conference on Knowledge Discovery and Data Mining*, pages 207–210, Newport Beach, California, August 1997.

[144] R. M. Karp and M. O. Rabin. Efficient randomized pattern–matching algorithms. Technical report, Harvard University, 1984.

[145] G. Karypis, E.-H. Han, and V. Kumar. CHAMELEON: A hierarchical clustering algorithm using dynamic modeling. *IEEE Computer*, 32:68–75, 1999.

[146] L. Kaufman and P. J. Rousseeuw. *Finding Groups in Data: An Introduction to Cluster Analysis*. John Wiley & Sons, New York, New York, 1990.

[147] R. L. Kennedy, Y. Lee, B. V. Roy, C. D. Reed, and R. P. Lippman. *Solving Data Mining Problems Through Pattern Recognition*. Prentice Hall, Upper Saddle River, New Jersey, 1998.

[148] J. M. Kleinberg. Authoritative sources in a hyperlinked environment. In *Proceedings of the Annual ACM-SIAM Symposium on Discrete Algorithms*, pages 668–677, New York, New York, 1998.

[149] D. E. Knuth, J. H. Morris, Jr., and V. R. Pratt. Fast pattern matching in strings. *SIAM Journal on Computing*, 6(1):323–350, 1977.

[150] D. Konopnicki and O. Shmueli. W3QS: A query system for the World Wide Web. In *Proceedings of the 21st International Conference on Very Large Data Bases*, pages 54–65, Zurich, Switzerland, September 1995.

[151] H. F. Korth and A. Silberschatz. *Database System Concepts*. McGraw Hill, New York, New York, 1991.

[152] R. Kumar, P. Raghavan, S. Rajagopalan, and A. Tomkins. Trawling the Web for emerging cyber-communities. In *Proceedings of the 8th International World Wide Web Conference*, pages 403–415, Toronto, Canada, May 1999.

[153] Z. Lacroix, A. Sahuguet, and R. Chandrasekar. Information extraction and database techniques: A user-oriented approach to querying the Web.

In *Advanced Information Systems Engineering, 10th International Conference CAiSE'98*, pages 289–304, Pisa, Italy, June 1998.

[154] Z. Lacroix, A. Sahuguet, R. Chandrasekar, and B. Srinivas. A novel approach to query the Web. In *Proceedings of the ER97 Workshop on Conceptual Modeling for Multimedia Information Seeking*, Los Angeles, California, November 1997.

[155] L. V. Lakshmanan, F. Sadri, and I. N. Subramanian. A declarative language for querying and restructuring the Web. In *Proceedings of the 6th International Workshop on Research Issues in Data Engineering: Interoperability of Nontraditional Database Systems*, 1996.

[156] L. V. S. Lakshmanan, R. Ng, J. Han, and A. Pang. Optimization of constrained frequent set queries with 2-variable constraints. In *Proceedings of the 1999 ACM SIGMOD International Conference on Management of Data*, pages 157–168, Philadelphia, Pennsylvania, June 1999.

[157] L. S. Larkey and W. B. Croft. Combining classifiers in text categorization. In *Proceedings of the 19th Annual International ACM SIGIR Conference on Research and Development in Information Retrieval*, pages 289–297, Zurich, Switzerland, August 1996.

[158] R. R. Larson. Bibliometrics of the World Wide Web: An exploratory analysis of the intellectual structure of cyberspace. In *Proceedings of the 1996 Annual ASIS Meeting*, pages 71–78, 1996.

[159] S. L. Lauritzen. The EM algorithm for graphical association models with missing data. *Computational Statistics and Data Analysis*, 19:191–201, 1995.

[160] S. Lawrence. Context in Web search. *IEEE Data Engineering Bulletin*, 23(3):25–32, 2000.

[161] S. Lawrence and C. L. Giles. Context and page analysis for improved Web search. *IEEE Internet Computing*, 2(4):38–46, July/August 1998.

[162] S. Lawrence and C. L. Giles. Searching the World Wide Web. *Science*, 280(5360):98–100, April 1998.

[163] S. Lawrence and C. L. Giles. Accessibility of information on the Web. *Nature*, 400(6740):107–109, 1999.

[164] A. Layman, E. Jung, E. Maler, H. S. Thompson, J. Paoli, J. Tigue, N. H. Mikula, and S. D. Rose. XML-Data. Technical report, World Wide

Web Consortium, 1998. http://www.w3.org/TR/1998/NOTE-XML-data-0105/.

[165] B. Lent, R. Agrawal, and R. Srikant. Discovering trends in text databases. In *Proceedings of the 3rd International Conference on Knowledge Discovery and Data Mining*, pages 227–230, Newport Beach, California, August 1997.

[166] B. Lent, A. Swami, and J. Widom. Clustering association rules. In *Proceedings of the 13th International Conference on Data Engineering*, pages 220–231, Birmingham, England, April 1997.

[167] M. Lesk. Going digital. *Scientific American*, 58–60, March 1997.

[168] A. Y. Levy, A. Rajaraman, and J. J. Ordille. Querying heterogeneous information sources using source descriptions. In *Proceedings of the 22nd International Conference on Very Large Data Bases*, pages 54–65, Bombay, India, September 1996.

[169] M. Ley. Database systems and logic programming bibliography server. http://www.informatik.uni-trier.de/~ley/db/index.html.

[170] S.-H. Lin, C.-S. Shih, M. C. Chen, J.-M. Ho, M.-T. Ko, and Y.-M. Huang. Extracting classification knowledge of Internet documents with mining term associations: A semantic approach. In *Proceedings of the 21st Annual International ACM SIGIR Conference on Research and Development in Information Retrieval*, pages 241–248, Melbourne, Australia, August 1998.

[171] Log Analyzer by WebTrends. http://www.webtrends.com.

[172] Lycos. http://www.lycos.com.

[173] Lycos Fast MP3 Search. http://mp3.lycos.com.

[174] Lycos Pictures and Sounds. http://www.lycos.com/picturethis.

[175] J. MacQueen. Some methods for classification and analysis of multivariate observations. In *Proceedings of the 5th Berkeley Symposium on Math. Statist. Problems*, pages 281–297, 1967.

[176] U. Manber and G. Myers. Suffix arrays: A new method for on–line string searches. In *Proceedings of the ACM–SIAM Symposium on Discrete Algorithms*, pages 319–327, San Francisco, California, 1990.

[177] U. Manber, M. Smith, and B. Gopal. WebGlimpse: Combining browsing and searching. In *Proceedings of USENIX Technical Conference*, pages 195–206, Anaheim, California, January 1997.

[178] U. Manber and S. Wu. GLIMPSE: A tool to search through entire file systems. In *Proceedings of the USENIX Technical Conference*, pages 23–32, San Francisco, California, January 1994.

[179] H. Mannila and H. Toivonen. Discovering generalized episodes using minimal occurrences. In *Proceedings of the 2nd International Conference on Knowledge Discovery and Data Mining*, pages 146–151, Portland, Oregon, August 1996.

[180] H. Mannila, H. Toivonen, and A. I. Verkamo. Efficient algorithms for discovering association rules. In *Proceedings of the AAAI Workshop on Knowledge Discovery in Databases*, pages 181–192, Seattle, Washington, July 1994.

[181] O. A. McBryan. GENVL and WWWW: Tools for taming the Web. In *Proceedings of the 1st International World Wide Web Conference*, pages 79–90, 1994.

[182] A. McCallum and K. Nigam. A comparison of event models for naive Bayes text classification. In *Proceedings of the AAAI-98 Workshop on Learning for Text Categorization*, 1998.

[183] A. McCallum, K. Nigam, J. Rennie, and K. Seymore. A machine learning approach to building domain-specific search engines. In *Proceedings of the 16th International Joint Conference on Artificial Intelligence*, pages 662–667, Stockholm, Sweden, August 1999.

[184] E. M. McCreight. A space-economical suffix tree construction algorithm. *Communications of the ACM*, 23(2):262–272, 1976.

[185] J. McHugh, S. Abiteboul, R. Goldman, D. Quass, and J. Widom. Lore: A database management system for semistructured data. *SIGMOD Record*, 26(3):54–66, September 1997.

[186] S. Mehrotra, K. Chakrabarti, M. Ortega, Y. Rui, and T. S. Huang. Towards extending information retrieval techniques for multimedia retrieval. In *Proceedings of the 3rd International Workshop on Multimedia Information Systems*, pages 39–45, Como, Italy, September 1997.

[187] A. O. Mendelzon, G. A. Mihaila, and T. Milo. Querying the World Wide Web. *International Journal on Digital Libraries*, 1(1):54–67, April 1997.

[188] R. Meo, G. Psaila, and S. Ceri. A new SQL-like operator for mining association rules. In *Proceedings of the 22nd International Conference*

on Very Large Data Bases, pages 122–133, Bombay, India, September 1996.

[189] MetaCrawler. http://www.metacrawler.com.

[190] R. S. Michalski. A theory and methodology of inductive learning. In R. S. Michalski, J. G. Carbonell, and T. M. Mitchell, editors, *Machine Learning: An Artificial Intelligence Approach*, volume 1, pages 83–134, San Mateo, California, 1983. Morgan Kaufmann.

[191] R. S. Michalski, I. Brakto, and M. Kubat. *Machine Learning and Data Mining: Methods and Applications*. John Wiley & Sons, New York, New York, 1998.

[192] Midi Explorer. http://www.musicrobot.com.

[193] R. J. Miller and Y. Yang. Association rules over interval data. In *Proceedings of the 1997 ACM SIGMOD International Conference on Management of Data*, pages 452–461, Tucson, Arizona, May 1997.

[194] T. M. Mitchell. *An Introduction to Genetic Algorithms*. MIT Press, Cambridge, Massachusetts, 1996.

[195] T. M. Mitchell. *Machine Learning*. McGraw-Hill, New York, New York, 1997.

[196] B. Mobasher, R. Cooley, and J. Srivastava. Creating adaptive Web sites through usage-based clustering of URLs. In *Proceedings of the 1999 IEEE Knowledge and Data Engineering Exchange Workshop*, 1999.

[197] Mozilla. http://www.mozilla.org.

[198] MP3. http://www.mp3.com.

[199] S. Mukherjea and J. Cho. Automatically determining semantics for World Wide Web multimedia information retrieval. *Journal of Visual Languages and Computing*, 10:586–606, 1999.

[200] S. Mukherjea, K. Hirata, and Y. Hara. Towards a multimedia World Wide Web information retrieval engine. In *Proceedings of the 6th International World Wide Web Conference*, Santa Clara, California, April 1997.

[201] S. K. Murthy. Automatic construction of decision trees from data: A multi-disciplinary survey. *Data Mining and Knowledge Discovery*, 2:345–389, 1998.

[202] O. Nasraoui, H. Frigui, A. Joshi, and R. Krishnapuram. Mining Web access logs using relational competitive fuzzy clustering. In *Proceedings of*

the 8th International Fuzzy Systems Association World Congress, Taipei, Taiwan, 1999.

[203] G. Navarro. Improved approximate pattern matching on hypertext. In *Proceedings of LATIN '98: Theoretical Informatics, 3rd Latin American Symposium*, pages 352–357, Campinas, Brazil, 1998.

[204] NetAnalysis by NetGenesis. http://www.netgen.com.

[205] Netscape Directory. http://directory.netscape.com.

[206] R. Ng, L. V. S. Lakshmanan, J. Han, and A. Pang. Exploratory mining and pruning optimizations of constrained associations rules. In *Proceedings of the 1998 ACM SIGMOD International Conference on Management of Data*, pages 13–24, Seattle, Washington, June 1998.

[207] K. Nigam, A. McCallum, S. Thrun, and T. M. Mitchell. Learning to classify text from labeled and unlabeled documents. In *Proceedings of the 15th National Conference on Artificial Intelligence*, Madison, Wisconsin, 1998.

[208] Northern Light. http://www.northernlight.com.

[209] M. Ortega, Y. Rui, K. Chakrabarti, S. Mehrotra, and T. S. Huang. Supporting similarity queries in MARS. In *Proceedings of the 5th ACM International Conference on Multimedia*, pages 403–413, Seattle, Washington, November 1997.

[210] L. Page, S. Brin, R. Motwani, and T. Winograd. The PageRank citation ranking: Bringing order to the Web. In *Proceedings of the 7th International World Wide Web Conference*, pages 161–172, Brisbane, Australia, April 1998.

[211] Z. Pawlak. *Rough Sets, Theoretical Aspects of Reasoning about Data.* Kluwer Academic Publishers, Norwell, Massachusetts, 1991.

[212] J. Pearl. *Probabilistic Reasoning in Intelligent Systems.* Morgan Kaufmann, Palo Alto, California, 1988.

[213] G. Piatetsky-Shapiro and W. J. Frawley, editors. *Knowledge Discovery in Databases.* AAAI/MIT Press, Cambridge, Massachusetts, 1991.

[214] R. W. Picard and M. Stonebraker. Vision texture for annotation. *ACM Journal of Multimedia Systems*, 3(1):3–14, 1995.

[215] B. Pinkerton. Finding what people want: Experiences with the WebCrawler. In *Proceedings of the 2nd International World Wide Web Conference*, pages 7–18, Chicago, Illinois, October 1994.

[216] P. Pirolli, J. Pitkow, and R. Rao. Silk from a sow's ear: Extracting usable structures from the Web. In *Proceedings of the 1996 Conference on Human Factors in Computing Systems*, pages 118–125, Vancouver, British Columbia, Canada, 1996.

[217] J. Pitkow. In search of reliable usage data on the WWW. In *Proceedings of the 6th International World Wide Web Conference*, Santa Clara, California, April 1997.

[218] D. Pyle. *Data Preparation for Data Mining*. Morgan Kaufmann, San Francisco, California, 1999.

[219] J. R. Quinlan. *C4.5: Programs for Machine Learning*. Morgan Kaufmann, San Francisco, California, 1993.

[220] M. Rajman and R. Besançon. Text mining: Natural language techniques and text mining applications. In *Proceedings of the 7th IFIP 2.6 Working Conference on Database Semantics*, Leysin, Switzerland, October 1997.

[221] R. Ramakrishnan and J. Gehrke. *Database Management Systems*. McGraw-Hill, New York, New York, 1999.

[222] E. J. Ray, D. S. Ray, and R. Seltzer. *The AltaVista Search Revolution*. Osborne/McGraw-Hill, Berkeley, California, 1998.

[223] J. Rennie and A. McCallum. Using reinforcement learning to spider the Web efficiently. In *Proceedings of the 16th International Conference on Machine Learning*, Bled, Slovenia, June 1999.

[224] C. J. Rijsbergen. *Information Retrieval*. Butterworths, Ontario, Canada, 1979.

[225] N. C. Rowe. Using local optimality criteria for efficient information retrieval with redundant information filters. *ACM Transactions on Information Systems*, 14(2):138–174, April 1996.

[226] N. C. Rowe and B. Frew. Automatic caption localization for photographs on World Wide Web pages. *Information Processing and Management*, 34(1):95–107, 1998.

[227] Y. Rubner and C. Tomasi. Coalescing texture description. In *Proceedings of the ARPA Image Understanding Workshop*, pages 927–936, 1996.

[228] G. Salton. *Automatic Text Processing: The Transformation, Analysis, and Retrieval of Information by Computer*. Addison–Wesley, Reading, Massachusetts, 1989.

[229] G. Salton and C. Buckley. Term-weighting approaches in automatic retrieval. *Information Processing and Management*, 15(1):8–36, 1988.

[230] G. Salton and M. E. Lesk. *Introduction to Modern Information Retrieval*. McGraw–Hill, New York, New York, 1983.

[231] SavvySearch. http://www.savvysearch.com.

[232] R. E. Schapire, Y. Singer, and A. Singhal. Boosting and Rocchio applied to text filtering. In *Proceedings of the 21st Annual International ACM SIGIR Conference on Research and Development in Information Retrieval*, pages 215–223, Melbourne, Australia, August 1998.

[233] Scour. http://www.scour.net.

[234] Search Engine Watch. http://www.searchenginewatch.com.

[235] E. Selberg and O. Etzioni. Multi-service search and comparison using the MetaCrawler. In *Proceedings of the 4th International World Wide Web Conference*, Boston, Massachusetts, December 1995.

[236] E. Selberg and O. Etzioni. The MetaCrawler architecture for resource aggregation on the Web. *IEEE Expert*, 12(1):11–14, January/February 1997.

[237] P. Sellers. The theory and computation of evolutionary distances: Pattern recognition. *Journal of Algorithms*, 6:132–137, 1980.

[238] C. Shahabi, A. M. Zarkesh, J. Abidi, and V. Shah. Knowledge discovery from user's Web-page navigation. In *Proceedings of the 7th IEEE International Workshop on Research Issues in Data Engineering*, pages 20–29, 1997.

[239] J. W. Shavlik and T. G. Dietterich. *Readings in Machine Learning*. Morgan Kaufmann, San Mateo, California, 1990.

[240] G. Sheikholeslami, S. Chatterjee, and A. Zhang. WaveCluster: A multiresolution clustering approach for very large spatial databases. In *Proceedings of the 24th International Conference on Very Large Data Bases*, New York, New York, August 1998.

[241] SherlockHound. http://www.sherlockhound.com.

[242] J. R. Smith and S.-F. Chang. Searching for images and videos on the World-Wide-Web. Technical report, Columbia University, 1996.

[243] J. R. Smith and S.-F. Chang. Tools and techniques for color image retrieval. In *Proceedings of the IS & T/SPIE*, pages 426–437, San Jose, California, March 1996.

[244] Solvent Alternatives Guide-SAGE. http://clean.rti.org.

[245] Sound Crawler. http://www.soundcrawler.com.

[246] M. Spiliopoulou. The laborious way from data mining to Web mining. *International Journal of Computing Systems, Science and Engineering*, 14:113–126, March 1999.

[247] M. Spiliopoulou, L. C. Faulstich, and K. Winkler. A data miner analyzing the navigational behaviour of Web users. In *Proceedings of the Workshop on Machine Learning in User Modeling of the ACAI99*, Greece, July 1999.

[248] Squid. http://squid.nlanr.net/squid.

[249] R. Srihari. Automatic indexing and content-based retrieval of captioned images. *IEEE Computer*, 28(9):49–56, 1995.

[250] R. Srikant and R. Agrawal. Mining generalized association rules. In *Proceedings of the 21st International Conference on Very Large Data Bases*, pages 407–419, Zurich, Switzerland, September 1995.

[251] R. Srikant and R. Agrawal. Mining sequential patterns: Generalizations and performance improvements. In *Proceedings of the 5th International Conference on Extending Database Technology*, pages 3–17, 1996.

[252] J. Srivastava, R. Cooley, M. Deshpande, and P.-N. Tan. Web usage mining: Discovery and applications of usage pattern from Web data. *SIGKDD Explorations*, 1(2):1–12, 2000.

[253] Stream Search. http://www.streamsearch.com.

[254] M. J. Swain and D. H. Ballard. Color indexing. *International Journal of Computer Vision*, 7(1):11–32, 1991.

[255] M. J. Swain, C. Frankel, and V. Athitsos. WebSeer: An image search engine for the World Wide Web. Technical report, Department of Computer Science, University of Chicago, 1996.

[256] H. Tamura and T. Yamawaki. Texture features corresponding to visual perception. *IEEE Transactions on Systems, Man, and Cybernetics*, 6(4):460–473, 1979.

[257] S.-H. Teng, Q. Lu, M. Eichstaedt, D. Ford, and T. Lehman. Collaborative Web crawling: Information gathering/processing over Internet.

In *Proceedings of the 32nd Hawaii International Conference on System Sciences*, pages 1–12, Maui, Hawaii, 1999.

[258] E. Ukkonen. Constructing suffix trees on-line in linear time. *Algorithmica*, 14(3):249–260, 1995.

[259] U.S. Patent and Trademark Office. http://www.uspto.gov.

[260] Q. Vu and W.-S. Li. Exploring link topology for associating Web pages. Unpublished Manuscript.

[261] J. T. L. Wang, B. A. Shapiro, and D. Shasha, editors. *Pattern Discovery in Biomolecular Data: Tools, Techniques and Applications*. Oxford University Press, New York, New York, 1999.

[262] W. Wang, J. Yang, and R. Muntz. STING: A statistical information grid approach to spatial data mining. In *Proceedings of the 23rd International Conference on Very Large Data Bases*, Athens, Greece, August 1997.

[263] Web Usage Characterization Activity. http://www.w3c.org/WCA.

[264] WebCrawler. http://www.webcrawler.com.

[265] WebSeek. http://disney.ctr.columbia.edu/webseek/.

[266] WebSeer. http://infolab.cs.uchicago.edu/webseer/.

[267] S. M. Weiss and N. Indurkhya. *Predictive Data Mining*. Morgan Kaufmann, San Francisco, California, 1998.

[268] S. M. Weiss and C. A. Kulikowski. *Computer Systems That Learn: Classification and Prediction Methods from Statistics, Neural Nets, Machine Learning, and Experts Systems*. Morgan Kaufmann, San Francisco, California, 1991.

[269] C. Westphal and T. Blaxton. *Data Mining Solutions: Methods and Tools for Solving Real-World Problems*. John Wiley & Sons, New York, New York, 1998.

[270] H. D. White and K. W. McCain. Bibliometrics. In *Annual Review of Information Science and Technology*, volume 24, pages 119–186, Elsevier, Amsterdam, 1989.

[271] R. Willett. Recent trends in hierarchical document clustering: A critical review. *Information Processing Management*, 25(5):465–476, 1988.

[272] I. H. Witten, A. Moffat, and T. C. Bell. *Managing Gigabytes: Compressing and Indexing Documents and Images*. Van Nostrand Reinhold, San Francisco, California, 2nd edition, 1999.

[273] World Wide Web Consortium (W3C). http://www.w3c.org.

[274] S. Wu and U. Manber. Fast text searching allowing errors. *Communications of the ACM*, 35(10):83–91, 1992.

[275] Yahoo! http://www.yahoo.com.

[276] Yahoo! Image Surf. http://isurf.yahoo.com.

[277] T. Yan, M. Jacobsen, H. Garcia-Molina, and U. Dayal. From user access patterns to dynamic hypertext linking. In *Proceedings of the 5th International World Wide Web Conference*, Paris, France, May 1996.

[278] Y. Yang, T. Ault, T. Pierce, and C. W. Lattimer. Improving text categorization methods for event tracking. In *Proceedings of the 23rd Annual International ACM SIGIR Conference on Research and Development in Information Retrieval*, pages 65–72, Athens, Greece, July 2000.

[279] Y. Yang, T. Pierce, and J. Carbonell. A study on retrospective and on-line event detection. In *Proceedings of the 21st Annual International ACM SIGIR Conference on Research and Development in Information Retrieval*, pages 28–36, Melbourne, Australia, August 1998.

[280] J. Yi and N. Sundaresan. Mining the Web for acronyms using the duality of patterns and relations. In *Proceedings of the 2nd ACM CIKM Workshop on Web Information and Data Management*, pages 48–52, Kansas City, Missouri, 1999.

[281] K. Yoda, T. Fukuda, Y. Morimoto, S. Morishita, and T. Tokuyama. Computing optimized rectilinear regions for association rules. In *Proceedings of the 3rd International Conference on Knowledge Discovery and Data Mining*, pages 96–103, Newport Beach, California, August 1997.

[282] L. A. Zadeh. Fuzzy sets. *Information and Control*, 8:338–353, 1965.

[283] O. R. Zaïane, M. Xin, and J. Han. Discovering Web access patterns and trends by applying OLAP and data mining technology on Web logs. In *Proceedings of Advances in Digital Libraries Conference*, Santa Barbara, California, 1998.

[284] K. Zhang, D. Shasha, and J. T. L. Wang. Approximate tree matching in the presence of variable length don't cares. *Journal of Algorithms*, 16(1):33–66, 1994.

[285] T. Zhang, R. Ramakrishnan, and M. Livny. BIRCH: An efficient data clustering method for very large databases. In *Proceedings of the 1996*

ACM SIGMOD International Conference on Management of Data, pages 103–114, Montreal, Canada, June 1996.

[286] W. Ziarko. *Rough Sets, Fuzzy Sets and Knowledge Discovery*. Springer-Verlag, New York, New York, 1994.

Index

About the Authors

George Chang is an Assistant Professor in the Mathematics and Computer Science Department at Kean University. He received his Ph.D. and M.S. in computer and information science from the New Jersey Institute of Technology in 2001 and 1995; and B.S. in computer science and applied mathematics and statistics from the State University of New York at Stony Brook in 1994. Dr. Chang was a Special Lecturer in the Computer and Information Science Department at the New Jersey Institute of Technology before joining Kean University in 1999. His research interests include databases, information retrieval, Web mining, and mobile/wireless application development.

Marcus J. Healey received his M.B.A. from Rider University with a concentration in finance; his M.S. is in chemical and biochemical engineering from Rutgers University; his Ph.D. and M.S. in environmental science are from Cook College, Rutgers University and his B.A. in biology is from University of Pennsylvania. He was the former Director of the New Jersey Program for Information Ecology and Sustainability at the New Jersey Institute of Technology. Dr. Healey has authored over 50 publications, presentations, and reports in scientific journals, conference proceedings, and technical reports. His primary interests are in the evolving world of Internet-based commerce, information systems, and writing about the environmental management business interface.

James A. M. McHugh received his A.B. in mathematics (with a minor in philosophy) from Fordham University in 1965 and the Ph.D. degree in applied mathematics from the Courant Institute of Mathematical Sciences, New York University in 1970, where he completed his thesis under National Academy of Science Member J. Keller. He has been a Member of Technical Staff at Bell Telephone Laboratories, Wave Propagation Laboratory, Director of the Ph.D. Program in Computer Science, and Acting Chair of the Computer and Information Science Department at the New Jersey Institute of Technology. Dr. McHugh has published over 35 papers in conference proceedings, books, and journals, and is the author of the book *Algorithmic Graph*

Theory (Prentice-Hall, 1989). Dr. McHugh's research interests include algorithmic graph, parallel algorithms, design and analysis of algorithms, pattern recognition, mathematical analysis and modelling, computer-aided problem-solving, and Web-based applications. Currently, Dr. McHugh is Full Professor in the Computer and Information Science Department at the New Jersey Institute of Technology.

Jason T. L. Wang received the B.S. degree in mathematics from National Taiwan University and the Ph.D. degree in computer science from the Courant Institute of Mathematical Sciences, New York University. Currently, he is Full Professor in the Computer and Information Science Department at the New Jersey Institute of Technology and Director of the University's Data and Knowledge Engineering Laboratory. Dr. Wang's research interests include data mining and databases, pattern analysis, computational biology, and information retrieval on the Internet. He has published 100 papers in conference proceedings, books, and journals. Dr. Wang is an editor and author of the book *Pattern Discovery in Biomolecular Data* (Oxford University Press), an associate editor of *Knowledge and Information Systems* (Springer-Verlag), on the Editorial Advisory Board of *Information Systems* (Pergamon Press), and a guest coeditor of the special issue on biocomputing of *International Journal of Artificial Intelligence Tools* (World Scientific). He is a member of New York Academy of Sciences, ACM, IEEE, AAAI, and SIAM.